soberevolution

evolve into sobriety and recover your alcoholic marriage

Matt Salis, with Sheri Salis

soberevolution

evolve into sobriety and recover your alcoholic marriage

Published by **Stone Soup Publishing**
Denver, Colorado
StoneSoupPublishing.org

Author's note: All events described in this book are real. Names of certain characters have been changed. The advice contained in this book is entirely the opinion of the author and should not be construed as medical advice. Alcoholism is a serious disease, and a medical detox conducted by medical professionals is often required for the safety of the patient to avoid seizures, other medical complications, and even death.

Library of Congress Cataloging-in-Publication Data is available upon request.

ISBN: 978-1-7353353-0-8 (Paperback)
ISBN: 978-1-7353353-1-5 (Hardcover)

BISAC Category: SELF-HELP / Substance Abuse & Addiction / Alcohol
Editing & Design by Julie Balsiger.

Quantity Purchases: Schools, companies, professional groups, clubs and other organizations may qualify for special terms when ordering quantities of this title. For information, email matt@SoberAndUnashamed.com

Printed in the United States of America

soberevolution

evolve into sobriety and recover your alcoholic marriage

For our parents.

*Who, despite having a lot of the blame
pointed in their direction, love us unconditionally
and have supported us unwaveringly.*

We thank and love them.

Prelude 1

Introduction 7

Part One | spiraling into alcoholism

Chapter 1:   alcoholic destiny 18
Chapter 2:   diabolical mind 31
Chapter 3:   decade of demise 44
Chapter 4:   love and alcoholism can't coexist 60
Chapter 5:   selfish pain 73

Part Two | evolving into sobriety

Chapter 6:   alcoholic monster 84
Chapter 7:   popular misperception 95
Chapter 8:   surviving the witching hour 111
Chapter 9:   rewiring your cranial supercomputer 123
Chapter 10: what you eat can cure you 139
Chapter 11: building sobriety muscles 151
Chapter 12: the power of vulnerability 162

Part Three | recovering a marriage

Chapter 13: almost tragic 176
Chapter 14: healing the wounds 189
Chapter 15: drowning intimacy 201
Chapter 16: evolve insecurity into instinct 216

Acknowledgments 226

About the author 227

| prelude

The transition from restless sleep to the panic of consciousness was as subtle as an electrical shock. My eyes sprang open, and I could feel my rapid heartbeat in my throat. I was drenched with sweat as I blinked the red blur on my bedside table into focus. It was 3:07 a.m., and the rush of terror flowed from my brain down my body and out to the tips of my fingers and toes.

Again! I had done it again!

It was a Monday morning, and too early to be wide awake and paralyzed with the anxiety of another failed attempt to control my drinking. I was dehydrated and my muscles ached from tension and poor sleep. But those conditions were minor inconveniences compared to the mental anguish resulting from my Sunday night alcoholic implosion.
It had all started innocently enough. But, doesn't it always?

As I sat in church listening to the sermon, I had a rare and fleeting sense of peacefulness. My work was done for the week. My four kids had no Sunday afternoon activities for which my wife, Sheri, and I had to serve as drivers. A little spiritual connection followed by an afternoon of relaxation awaited.

Calm and restful moments like that one were elusive for me. My mind was constantly whirling with evaluations of my recent performance, and analysis of plans for the future. It was a problem, really. Stopping the cranial pandemonium was a challenge. That day, as I tried to melt into the church pew, I looked forward to a few beers and zoning out, hoping my relentlessly active mind would cooperate.

I call it chaotic mind syndrome, and one of alcohol's superpowers is to make it go away. A lot of people think drinking alcohol is a complementary accent to relaxation. In reality, for me and for millions, we learn to use alcohol to suffocate our brains enough to find temporary relief from the chaos. What we don't understand is that it is alcohol that fuels the chaos in the first place. The remedy is the cause and continuing the cycle can only lead to devastating consequences.

I tried to manage the last 10 years of my drinking—my decade of active alcoholism—with a series of different rules I employed to contain my consumption. On that particular Sunday, my rules restricted my intake to six India pale ales. To ensure I would stick to my limit, I had only six cold beers in the refrigerator while the rest of my bounty was stored at room temperature.

On about the third deliciously bitter IPA, I entered the danger zone. The feeling of euphoria was engulfing, and the chaos in my mind had drifted into a state of hibernation. I felt invincible. The only challenge that remained was stopping after six and finding satisfaction in my allotted quantity of hops and barley. I was notorious for succumbing to "fuck it" moments when in the danger zone. When the desire to continue to drink overwhelmed my commitment to my self-imposed restriction, all bets were off—and the evening was sure to end badly.

Success, for a high-functioning alcoholic like me, was defined by sticking to my rules and remaining mindful of the people and things around me. I had finished my six-pack of potent, high-alcohol beer when my 14-year-old daughter called from the theater to tell me her friends all wanted to go to dinner after the movie. A reasonable reaction from my alcohol-soaked mind was out of the question. She was asking to get a burger with half a dozen of her best friends and a couple of their moms. She was not calling to tell me she was going to smoke weed with a boy I'd never met. Her request was as innocent as my reaction was exaggerated. I reluctantly agreed, but not without giving my oldest daughter, with an impeccable track record for responsibility and sound decision making, a verbal thrashing she did not deserve.

I ended the call and went straight for my stash of warm beers in the basement. How could I possibly have been expected to obey my own rules when the family plans for the evening had been so needlessly disrupted? I had planned to sulk around the house post-beer consumption, then go to bed quietly with little to no interaction with my children. Now, one of my kids would not be there for me to ignore. What an outrage. Fuck it! I needed a drink.

My wife knew my six-beer rule, but I didn't think she had been counting beers on that particular Sunday. She would have been appalled, had she known I was now guzzling warm beers to chase the relief I had experienced earlier in the day. Appalled, but not surprised. She would have been furious, however, had she caught me sneaking gulps of warm gin from the bottle in the kitchen pantry. Hard alcohol was off limits, per my then-current iteration of my drinking rules, so I had to be very careful as I took greedy, desperate pulls from the medicating Tanqueray bottle.

And that was the last thing I remembered from the evening: sneaking into the kitchen pantry four, five, maybe six times to ease the pain of restriction and self-inflicted disappointment. With each visit, I took the biggest gulp my body would accept without reversing the flow, as I tried to kill the anxiety and depression that emerged to replace the euphoria of the afternoon's first couple of beers.

The next thing I knew, it was 3:07 a.m., and I was in a full-blown panic attack. The workday was almost upon me, and I hadn't gotten a minute's rest (passing out for a few hours is a terrible replacement for restorative sleep). The drink I had used to subdue my swirling thoughts hours earlier brought the chaos raging back, more explosive and consuming than ever. I felt death creeping toward me, and I was defenseless to avoid it. It was like running in a dream while the monster continued to gain ground. Survival seemed impossible.

I woke my wife, not out of anger or cruelty, but because I did not know what else to do. She was all too familiar with the drill. She tried to use calming words and assure me my behavior had not set any new standards for drunken debauchery. She was well-versed on swimming the shark-infested seas without chumming the water.

She tried unsuccessfully to hide her ambivalence toward the whole episode. Even when I told her I felt like I was dying, she didn't have any love or compassion left to allow her to feign concern for my survival. So many years of the same story on different nights had wrung the empathy right out of her. As she laid in the quiet dark trying to talk me back to sleep, her concern was not for me. She was trying to keep me from turning to the only other form of self-medication she was dreadfully accustomed to me seeking. She was trying to say soothing words that would keep me from begging for sex in the tiny pre-dawn hours.

As in so many panic-stricken, middle-of-the-night moments of the past, I rolled toward my wife and told her I

needed relief from the demons that consumed me. I asked
her to take off her pajama bottoms and show me the physical
love that had long since left the marriage emotionally. Just as
I'd used the gin bottle the night before, I wanted to use her
body to find temporary comfort from my all-consuming pain.

Sheri politely declined, citing the hour and her need for
sleep. I begged. She turned away, and I insisted. She held the
covers tight around her body as I sobbed and pleaded.

That's when Sheri did the most loving and generous thing
imaginable. She agreed to let me have sex with her lifeless
body. She agreed not out of love for me—that emotion had
been so abused and battered that it laid dormant at the
bottom of her soul. She rolled over, removed her underwear
and spread her legs to keep me quiet and let her four babies
sleep. Sheri was completely done being a loving wife, but she
would never cease to be a loving mother. She agreed with my
despicable request so our four children wouldn't wake up to
their father's slobbery cries of self-inflicted terror.

Later that still-early morning, I stared at my puffy face
and blood-shot eyes in the bathroom mirror. Like everything
else, that moment leaning over the sink was one that had
repeated itself too many times to count. I had to quit. Not
slow down or impose new rules—I had to stop drinking
alcohol forever. The pain was too strong and deep. I was not
thinking about the pain I was inflicting on my wife. I wasn't
worried about the curt words and variable temperament to
which I was subjecting my kids. I was selfishly fixated on my
own pain. I had lost the will to live.

That morning, I didn't recognize the cowering shell of a
man staring back at me in the mirror. I knew the nightmare
had to end. I knew how challenging it would be to stop
drinking alcohol, but I was completely backed into a corner,

and I had no choice but to make it over the seemingly insurmountable hump to lasting sobriety.

What my self-absorbed mind could not yet comprehend was how hard it would be to save our marriage. I knew I had to get sober. I was so naive. I thought sobriety would fix our lives.

Sobriety doesn't heal anything. Sobriety just rips off the bandages and exposes the wounds we slowly inflict by decades of abusive drinking.

So, I would drink no more. I thought the pain was over. Little did I know, the misery and anguish were just beginning.

Welcome to my sobriety, and the recovery of our alcoholic marriage.

This is a love story.

It is the story of the love that developed between me and my wife. And, my love for alcohol.

It is also the story of how a loving relationship and alcoholism can't coexist. They just can't. One will destroy the other—every single time.

I met my wife, Sheri, in college, and drinking soothed the awkwardness of learning to know each other. Alcohol sped things along. It encouraged us to charge forward together, where caution may have been advisable. Booze lowered our inhibitions and poured gasoline on a smoldering physical relationship. Alcohol drew us together like magnets and made our future together inevitable.

But alcohol also made us greedy and selfish. It encouraged us to push boundaries that should have been respected and caused imaginary conflict that didn't really exist. We argued about ridiculous things—things so trivial that we often couldn't remember what we were fighting about as the booze fueled the anger. We wounded one another even as we were falling in love with each other.

After college, Sheri matured, and her drinking dissipated. She slowed down, both as a natural condition of adulthood, and because my overconsumption began to repulse her. The more I drank, the less she wanted to drink. And, the more I drank, the less she wanted to be around me.

Sheri's love for me started to wane. Just as alcohol had been responsible for turning a spark into a flame, it was later the single factor that caused her to question her decision to bond her life to mine. She always knew I loved her, but she started to understand that I loved my precious drink even more. No one wants to be second in a marriage. Sheri, my devoted wife, and the loving mother of our four kids, didn't deserve that.

This is the story of conquering the most difficult challenges of our lives. I'm talking, of course, about my recovery from alcoholism. Finding permanent sobriety was arduous and painful. But I'm also talking about recovering our marriage—about choosing each other over addiction—and working together to fight our way back to love.

Probably the most important lesson of our lives was learning that sobriety doesn't fix anything. Sobriety only pulls back the bandages of alcoholism—exposing the festering wounds inflicted over years and decades of abusive drinking. The mandatory work for saving our marriage required determination, humility and patience like nothing we'd ever experienced. Sobriety was only the first, necessary step.

Sobriety doesn't fix anything, but it is a prerequisite.

This is a story told in three parts: first, I explain how two happy, eager, motivated, morally sound, hard-working and loving people found themselves in an alcoholic marriage. Then, I describe my 10-year battle with active alcoholism, including everything I learned about finding permanent sobriety. Last, I detail the stages involved in what I have come to refer to as a relationship recovery cycle—moving from the pain of resentment to the joy of love and intimacy.

Our story builds from how we got stuck, to how we rooted out the evil, then finally, to how we found love again. I tell the story using my own words and from my perspective, but Sheri contributed to every single page. She shared her memories, her feelings and all her pain, so we could get the story right. She edited each chapter for veracity and emotional sentiment and ensured that when I represented her side of the story, I did so accurately. This is our story, written from my point of view, but told together.

This is a story that has to be told—not just as a part of the healing of our marriage, or to help others find freedom from addiction and reconciliation for their relationships—but also to help defeat the stigma associated with alcoholism. There are over 15 million alcoholics in the United States. That is slightly more than the number of people afflicted with cancer. The World Health Organization estimates that three million people die every year from alcohol-related causes. Three million. This isn't a disease that deserves to be talked about in hushed whispers and condescending tones. Alcoholism has never received the attention it deserves, maybe because it hits a little too close to home for all of us, and the associated shame is just too ripe and tangible.

Alongside many other recovery warriors who are telling their stories, it is my goal to destigmatize the epidemic of alcoholism. We've tried the, "ignore it and hope it goes away," strategy without success. It's time to shout about the damage done by one of the world's most highly addictive substances.

January 10, 2018 was the best day of my life. That's not my wedding day or the birth date of any of my children. It's not my sobriety date, either. That's the day I sent over 3,000 emails to everyone who had ever given me their contact

information, explaining that I was a high-functioning
alcoholic, and that I had been sober for one year.

January 9th was the most terrifying day of my life. I was
convinced I would be fired from my job, and I anticipated all
the negative feedback I would receive when I admitted my
affliction. It took every bit of courage I could muster to push
the send button on the morning of the 10th. My decision to
be open about my disease was rewarded in ways I never
imagined possible.

First, I was not fired from my job. In fact, I later learned
my boss was relieved to receive an email about a problem
that I had already solved. It contrasted well with the rest of
his inbox full of fires that required his attention. It was such a
non-issue at work, that a year later, my boss didn't even
remember the email I had been so terrified to send.

As for friends and family, the response and support I
received was completely overwhelming. While everyone,
outside of my immediate and closest family, was shocked (we
high-functioning alcoholics exert incredible effort to hide our
predilection), the warmth and encouragement I felt from my
unsuspecting loved ones was tremendous. Some of my
drinking buddies were among the most authentically excited
that I had taken such a healthy step. I'm sure there are event
invitations that no longer come my way, and I know my
openness causes discomfort for some in my circle who
internally question their own relationship with alcohol. But
none of that is my problem. I have never heard a negative
word about my admission.

The really magical part of my decision to shout about my
sobriety is how it has transformed casual, throw-away
relationships with acquaintances, neighbors and distant
friends into bonds of shared pain and redemption. I'm not

just talking about other alcoholics. So many people who I barely knew before heard the authenticity of my message and wanted to get to know me better. People are drawn to vulnerability. Honesty is attractive in ways that a blemish-free reputation never can be. To say that coming out about my alcoholism and recovery was life-changing is an enormous understatement.

The most transformational aspect of my decision to recover out loud is how it solidified the decision itself. I told everyone I knew that alcohol was killing me and destroying my family. Who was going to drink with me after that? Once I sent those emails, there was no going back. Sobriety was my sealed destiny. From that day forward, temptation and cravings were powerless over me. I couldn't drink if I wanted to.

No amount of deceit and denial that I had wielded so successfully as an active alcoholic would be enough to hide my drinking once I had pointed a spotlight in my own face. It was over. My drinking days were done.

As miraculous as my permanent sobriety was, my work was just beginning. In early recovery, I expected sobriety to improve my marriage. I was shocked to find that the relationship with my wife was getting worse.

A marriage has the potential to be the closest and most impactful relationship of our lives. It should not have surprised me that the damage done to my marriage by my active alcoholism was so profound and crippling. It should not have surprised me, but it did. My wife was skeptical about my sobriety as I had tried and failed to quit drinking so many times before.

She felt like her pain was being ignored as my focus was singular and intense on finding relief from cravings and temptation to drink. Sheri wanted to support me, but there was no way she was lowering her guard and showing any vulnerability or weakness. The wall of resentment we had built between us in reaction to my alcoholism was tall and strong, and my enthusiastic commitment to sobriety was not going to bring it down any time soon.

Alcoholism is a diabolical disease. Many marriages adapt to the trauma and disappointment that addiction delivers to the relationship. Protecting the intimate truth of being married to an alcoholic becomes part of the family legacy of lies and denials. Many couples avoid divorce when struggling to survive high-functioning alcoholism. Because of the shame of failure and exposure of the root cause, they stay married. They may also stay intoxicated and emotionally abused and adapt to a loveless relationship because the alternative is cloaked in stigma.

A 2014 study conducted at the University of Michigan, found a 50 percent divorce rate for alcoholic marriages, 20 percent higher than marriages where alcohol abuse was not a problem. There is no surprise that addiction to alcohol causes an increase in failed marriages, but I think they studied the wrong thing. I have never found statistics on the percentage of marriages that fail after alcohol has been removed from the marriage. That was not a subset of the University of Michigan study. As far as I can tell, it has never been researched. That's really too bad. The results from the Michigan study suggest, as has often been suggested in the addiction research community, that if you take away alcohol, things get better. That's simply not the case.

Since it has never been studied, my assertion relies on personal experience and the stories of so many others in the recovery community. I would be willing to wager that if active alcoholism results in a 20 percent increase in divorce rate, sobriety in a formerly alcoholic marriage probably has twice the impact. It wouldn't surprise me if alcoholic marriages dissolve at a 90 percent rate when the alcohol is removed for one or both spouses.

Recovering an alcoholic marriage is hard. Really hard. I don't think it has ever been studied because the truth would be so damning. If failure is imminent, then why even try? I think the message a study like that would send to many drinkers is that you might as well keep on drinking. Keep suffering and battling and living a loveless, despair-filled life. The truth might leave couples feeling doomed and hopeless.

But there is hope.

Sheri and I made it. And our marriage has reached a level of cooperation, understanding, trust, love and intimacy we never imagined. It's not like it was back in college when alcohol fueled our passion—it is much better. Surviving trauma permanently changes people. And when two people survive together, the resulting bond is unbreakable.

We read a lot of books and articles written by psychologists, addiction counselors and relationship therapists when we were trying to save our marriage in early sobriety from my alcoholism. The suggestions we found made sense, but they were too generic and unspecific and ultimately, the advice was ineffective for us in our efforts to improve our relationship. This book isn't about psychobabble and general recommendations for relationship improvement. If you are looking for a book based on scientific study or years of experience in a counseling practice, this book is not for you.

If you are looking for a man-bashing, divorce-promoting book to tell you that your alcoholic spouse is evil and incapable of repentance, this is not the book for you. If you want tips on sober dating or sober casual sex in an alcohol-filled world, this book is not for you. If you want confirmation that your life and your relationship is hopeless, and you are looking for permission to give up trying, this book is not for you.

If you have already made up your mind—if the flame is not just burning out, but it has been permanently extinguished by too many lies, too much abuse and too much time wasted in a wasted marriage—then I'm sorry, but there is nothing we can do for you. This book is not for you.

But if you have even a glimmer of hope, please keep reading.

If you want to quit drinking alcohol, but nothing you have tried has worked, this book is for you regardless of your relationship status. Before we tackle the topic of saving a marriage, we must save ourselves. If you are a high-functioning alcoholic, single or married, man or woman and you want to find freedom, I'm hopeful that my method of navigating early sobriety might resonate with you. I hope you keep reading.

If you are married to a high-functioning alcoholic, actively drinking or in sobriety, this book is for you. If you want your marriage to thrive, your partner will have to find sobriety. It is not a spiritual condition, nor is alcoholism a sign of weakness or immorality. It is a disease like cancer. If you are going to help your spouse find health, you need to understand the affliction. We will cover everything from brain chemistry and the patterns of the subconscious mind, to strategies for recovery and the benefits of recovering out loud. We can't fix something we don't understand, so we must learn about alcoholism before we can defeat it.

Like I said, sobriety is not a solution, but it is a prerequisite. If you are ready to learn about and beat alcoholism, this book is for you.

If you've successfully removed alcohol from your marriage, and your relationship is getting worse, this book is for you. After we understand how to find permanent sobriety, we must figure out how to pick up the pieces of our lives and rebuild. The marriage recovery cycle starts at resentment and ends at love and intimacy, but the journey is long and treacherous. If you want to know how we made it, how we found the courage, patience, trust, love and understanding to bridge the enormous divide my 25 years of heavy drinking created in our life together, we hope you'll keep reading.

This book is our story, a love story. It is raw and descriptive and emotional and painful. It is about standing at the fork in the road and choosing the more difficult path, over and over again. It is about finding lasting sobriety when it would have been easier, albeit deadly, to just keep drinking. It is about digging deep and working through the massive barriers to love, when we both probably deserved a fresh start without years of built-up resentments. It is about choosing the health of our children over the relief of leaving the pain and trauma behind. It is about the willingness to try again—and again, and again, and again—until we figured it out and the wounds began to heal.

This is our love story.

If you still have hope, this could be your love story, too.

spiraling into alcoholism

Part One

chapter 1 | alcoholic destiny

The 200-mph Beer Can

My father shook me awake in the dark, early morning hours
of Sunday, May 28, 1978. "Mom's sick. Do you want to go to
the race?" At age five, those were the best 10 words I had
ever heard. Well, maybe not the first two, but the next eight
had me bouncing out of bed. My parents attended the
Indianapolis 500 on the Sunday of Memorial Day Weekend
every year. Two tickets for two people. Now, one of them
was sick, and I was next in line for the throne at the center of
the auto racing universe.

If you're not an IndyCar fan, don't worry. This isn't a
book about auto racing. Pretend I was invited to the Final
Four, Les Misérables on its Broadway opening night, the
Super Bowl, or the Oscars. Whatever your jam, think of the
annual highlight. For a kid growing up in Southern Indiana,
the Indy 500 was Mecca. I was going to the race and with my
dad, who I emulated and revered as the pinnacle of
manliness.

Before we even made it to our seats, I was welcomed to
the cathedral of speed and the tabernacle of hops and barley
by a 16-ounce shower of beer. Some exuberant fan, who had
clearly imbibed his breakfast, spilled a full beer from the
grandstands above as we navigated to our assigned spots in
the bleachers. It was 9 a.m., and I smelled like a Texas
roadhouse at closing time. I would spend the next six hours
baking my liquid coating in the sun. My first Indy 500 was
sticky and bittersweet.

The truth is, I didn't mind my beer bath one bit. The energy and enthusiasm of the racing arena was electric, so a little collateral damage was not surprising. Besides, I smelled like my dad's favorite beverage. Even at age five, the smell of beer fostered thoughts of family and free time. And now, I was sitting in the middle of 300,000 people who would, with very few exceptions, spend the day guzzling beer like it was their birthright.

The Indianapolis Motor Speedway really is a special place. The Memorial Day Weekend race is one of our national treasures that should be experienced firsthand, whether you care about cars driving 220 miles per hour or not. As an adult, a business associate took me to a practice round for the Masters Golf Tournament once. That's another such place. Walking the grounds at Augusta in April feels like being in a fantasy world. The grass is a different color green than I've experienced before or since. Indy is a lot like that. The race is important, but in a lot of ways, it is secondary. The people, the pageantry and the patriotism are what keeps the mass of humanity coming back year after year. All of that, and, of course, the party. The Indy 500 really is just a two-and-a-half mile, oval-shaped keg party with a huge cover charge.

My parents' seats were on the outside of Turn 2. For many decades, including the late 70s, the inside of Turn 2 was referred to as, "the Snake Pit." That's where the serious partiers elevated drinking to a blood sport. Think about it for a minute. They were on the inside of a corner that cars would navigate at roughly 200 miles per hour. You don't have to be a geometry expert to understand that the race would be a blur from that vantage point, even if a person was sober. But trust me, no one in the Snake Pit has ever been sober. When you are 50 feet from the track, but can't see the race, you have to find other ways to occupy yourself. In the Snake Pit, they drank early and often until they were kicked out or carried out.

The dedication to intoxication was explained on the dozens of poster board signs that so eloquently demanded, "Show Us Your Tits!" The Snake Pit dwellers displayed the signs to the military members, the marching band, the legends of races past—and most enthusiastically to the queen of the Indianapolis 500 Festival and her court of princesses, as they paraded around the track before the race. The dignitaries ignored the Snake Pit requests without exception, so the hooligans turned their signs, and their insistent demands, on their own females (who were drinking whiskey from funnels at 10 a.m.), with a much better rate of success. The party in the Snake Pit was legendary, and it was a cornerstone of the Indy 500 experience. It was also the reason my dad brought binoculars.

When the cars took to the track, I was speechless as I spotted the bright red Budweiser car coming toward me out of Turn 1. A car painted like a can of my dad's beer was passing in front of me for the first of 200 plus times that day. It was magnificent. It stirred emotions of time spent with my hero, and I would cheer for it above the roar of the engines every time it came through the Short Chute on the south end of the track.

In 1978, Budweiser was sponsoring Mario Andretti, arguably the greatest race car driver in history. To this day I am a huge Andretti fan, having cheered for him, his son, his grandson and his nephew at the dozens of Indy 500s I have attended since my first race at age five. The Andrettis have delivered incalculable drama, excitement and (mostly) heartache for me and their thousands of other fans at Indy. In May of 1978, I didn't know I was starting a lifetime career of rooting for a legendary family. I was rooting for my dad's favorite beer. A blind, quadruple amputee could have been driving, and it wouldn't have made a difference to me.

That's the point, really. That's the point of this whole story. At age five, beer was an integral part of my persona. So much so that I didn't mind being drenched in beer and was transfixed for half a day by the speedy logo of one of the world's largest breweries. I didn't think of the Snake Pit as a den of debauchery. To the contrary, I was jealous of the fat and dirty men in cutoff jean shorts bouncing up and down with half-naked women perched on their shoulders. They paid a lot of money to be there. There is powerful influence in numbers, and there is no way that many people, each with an aluminum can permanently attached their hand, could have been wrong. I didn't just want to be with them, I wanted to be one of them. At age five, adulthood already held the promise of happiness and fellowship with a 12-ounce pop-top.

I sat next to my dad that entire glorious day. He was one of them. He fit in. He didn't scream at women to bare their breasts, and he didn't drive a car at 220 miles an hour, but he had his place. He had his six-pack of Bud that was his ticket to acceptance. He was welcomed into the massive tradition that was Indy in the month of May. There is no place on earth I would rather have been that day, and no person I would rather have been with. My dad taught me what Indy was all about. More importantly, he connected the dots of alcohol and adulthood, that day and every day.

By the end of my teen years, I was hoisting my own golden amber cans of maturity among the masses gathered on race day. I repeated that tradition annually for a couple of decades, until the reality of my predicament finally caught up to me, and I had to end my lifelong love affair with beer.

The first time I attended the Greatest Spectacle in Racing in sobriety was among the worst days of my life. There is nothing quite like squeezing into your seat with 300,000 other people and feeling overwhelmed by loneliness. The Snake Pit had been dispatched to my intoxicating memories of the races of my youth, so I didn't have a pile of drunken idiots to remind me I was glad to be sober. Nor did I have a gaggle of bare-breasted women to distract me from the shame of my sobriety. I was left feeling painfully aware of how little I had in common with so many people who looked and dressed just like me. All that was left for me was the racing. It turns out, I don't really like IndyCars as much as I thought I did. The race was just an excuse to gather with a quarter of a million or so strangers, and drink as much as my body would hold—and sometimes more, with embarrassing consequences.

But my love affair with alcohol started for me at such an impressionable and formative age in the spring of 1978. My hero, some well-spent advertising money and hundreds of thousands of influential strangers all pointed me in the same direction. I wasn't old enough yet to ride the school bus or sign my name in cursive, but the indoctrination was complete. I was an alcoholic before I took my first sip.

Sex and Drugs can Break My Bones, but Booze will Never Hurt Me

Alcohol remained on the forefront of my conscious mind, even as I was still many years away from the legal drinking age. My first sips came like so many from my generation: if I

brought my dad a beer on a Saturday afternoon, having
pulled off the tab and thrown it away, and having not spilled
any on the trip from the refrigerator to the back porch, I was
rewarded with a sip.

I think adults did that to see the pucker face kids would
make in repulsion. But I didn't make that face. I viewed the
bitter bite of the carbonated elixir as a sign that adult men
were tough. I figured that the thirst that only beer would
quench was just beyond my comprehension as a young boy. I
wanted those sips. I wanted them badly. I wanted to feel the
tingle of the thing I would someday grow to love.

The connections are so important to my alcoholic story.
The connection I made between alcohol and manhood was
profound and undisputed within my family, my circle of
friends and society as a whole. Nancy Reagan went to a lot of
effort to convince my friends and me to "Just Say No" to
drugs, but the First Lady was nowhere to be found in the fight
against teen drinking. Who am I kidding—there was no one
fighting against teen drinking back then. MADD (Mothers
Against Drunk Driving) was just gaining momentum when I
was a kid, so we were vaguely aware of the dangers of
drinking and driving.

But that message was drowned out by images of my father
driving us home from weekend neighborhood barbeques
after drinking beer after beer with the other men. He drove
even though my mother didn't have anything to drink at all.
The message that got through was that drunk driving was a
sad and stupid thing, but it was clearly someone else's
problem. It wasn't even receiving a moment's consideration
in my family. I don't ever remember a discussion about who
would take the wheel.

Besides the war on drugs (which completely ignored the deadliest drug of all), the other public health crisis of my youth was the AIDS epidemic. We were taught at an early age to wrap it up or die. I remember the fervor being much more serious in the homosexual community, but us horny little straight boys received no shortage of terrifying warnings about the lifesaving benefits of condoms. It wasn't much of a hard sell. None of my friends were really in the market for becoming parents in our teens, so a condom ring bulging from our wallets was a badge of honor.

As much as we made fun of the relentless PSAs about the dangers of drugs and AIDS, the messages were received because our role models, and society in general, did nothing to dispute them. Nobody wanted AIDS. In addition to the deadliness, that was the "gay disease." Even if contracted from unprotected heterosexual intercourse, you were assumed to be gay if you got AIDS. Nobody wanted any part of any of that.

It was the 1980s. Most Americans were close-minded and prejudiced. Homophobia was not just accepted, it was revered. The most popular show on television was Cheers, and I specifically remember an episode where all the regulars left the pub because of a single gay patron. The message from this show, set in a sports bar in Boston, was that drinking constantly was estimable—but being gay made you defective.

The same was true of drugs in my youthful era. Nancy said no, and there wasn't much argument from my little world of influence. We didn't sneak lines of cocaine from my parents' drug cabinet (because no such piece of furniture existed). But the abundance of the exotic bottles in the liquor cabinet were just begging to be relieved of some of their bounty.

And it wasn't just our parents. The parties of my teens were about beer and vodka. We knew a few kids who were doing LSD, and I smoked a joint once or twice in high school, but it just wasn't ever-present like booze. Besides, if we got caught drinking, we knew there would be consequences, but we knew Nancy wouldn't be mad at us. Drugs came with felonies and bad grades and a series of disastrous life choices.

Alcohol, on the other hand, was the prize for becoming an adult without getting a girl pregnant, contracting AIDS or doing time for drug possession.

The distinction could not have been clearer.

Sex and Alcohol—the Inextricable Connection

While it was universally agreed that teen pregnancy was to be avoided, the pregnancy-producing act was the throbbing naughty intention to be carried out at every possible opportunity. Sex and alcohol became the inextricably linked goals of each weekend in high school. In college, the goals remained the same and the barriers to success were much lower.

Shedding parental supervision was a game changer that made higher education a thirsty, naked free-for-all. Okay, it wasn't quite as bohemian as Woodstock. We wore button-down shirts, and usually wore condoms.

I was a business major in college. I learned about Generally Accepted Accounting Principles (GAAP). I learned about the supply and demand curve, and I learned that red and yellow are the most eye-catching colors to use in point-of-sale advertising. I learned that Volleyball 101 was the most fantastic way possible to fulfill a humanities credit requirement, and I learned to eat ramen noodles three meals a day because it left more money for beer, cigarettes and vodka.

But the most important lesson I learned in college was that if you wanted to get in a girl's pants, the plans had better include alcohol. I'm not talking about anything as sinister as date rape or even questionable consent. I'm talking about the shyness that plagues young adults and setting the scene in the only way we knew how. Weekends meant parties, and girls flocked to free beer like moths to a front porch light.

I wouldn't say the lines between a blossoming relationship with the opposite sex and drinking booze were blurred. There were no lines at all separating these two occupiers of 90 percent of our college-aged brains. Drinking with my buddies was a lot of fun. Throw in a round of showers and a stick of deodorant, and the possibilities for intoxicated female affection were endless.

While on a road trip with a bunch of guys to another college, I was laying on the basement floor of a fraternity next to one of my best friends. On the verge of passing out, my friend asked and answered his own question. "Do you know the only thing that could make this better, Matt? If we had some warm boobs to snuggle with right now." From that day forward, we called each other WB.

The point is, sometimes getting drunk was the desired result. But more often than not, alcohol was the prerequisite for sex, or even the start of a relationship with a girl. Alcohol wasn't an accessory like a fashionable handbag or a gold chain or a wallet with a condom ring. Alcohol was the first in a series of steps that occasionally resulted in a bra and underwear wadded up in a ball at the foot of my bed in the morning.

Just like my childhood world convinced me that alcohol was the reward of adulthood, booze was clearly defined as the only road leading to intimacy later in my young life. It was such a basic and fundamental lesson that it might as well have been on the syllabus on the first day of college.

Some things are difficult to unlearn. Price elasticity of commodity products is one of them. That you could afford to eat your weight at 10-cent-wings nights at BW3s is another. That companionship—you know, the kind with warm boobs—requires a stop at the liquor store, that one was seared into my cranium with frequency and determination.

But here's the thing, it's human nature to look for shortcuts and take the path of least resistance. We didn't drink and provide booze to girls because we were evil boys with demonic intentions. We injected alcohol into every social setting because it had a much-desired effect. Talking to a stranger of the opposite sex became infinitely easier for all involved. We bypassed the awkward "feeling each other out" stage and went straight to feeling each other up. We became intimate before we became friends. We were lusty and adventurous when we should have been cautious and inquisitive.

Stigma of Shame

Nothing has impacted the relationship with my wife more than alcohol has. Booze brought us together, then it nearly ripped us apart. First, we drank together, then I kept drinking and built a seemingly insurmountable wall of resentment. We did that. I did that. We have no one to blame but ourselves.

We had choices, and the ones we made resulted in sleepless, argument-filled nights, debilitating depression, destroyed trust and lasting trauma.

It is our fault. It is my fault. I get that. I own it.

But to ignore the influences that put us in the mess in which we found ourselves is to ignore reality. If we don't speak the truth, we doom the generations that come after us to the same consequences.

Sure, I chose to drink, but I didn't realize I had a choice to not drink. I entangled alcohol with every single romantic relationship in my life. I did that. But I didn't know any other way. I was reasonably well-behaved. I mostly did what I was told. That included adopting alcohol into my life as a foundational element. As a result, I made a nightmarish mess of a huge chunk of my regrettable life.

Alcoholism is a disease of shame shrouded in a stigma of deviance. But that's not who I was. I was a good boy who kissed his momma goodnight and tried to make his father proud. I got Bs in school, made friends easily and prayed to God to give me the answers. I had a good upbringing. I had a good moral compass. I knew right from wrong, and I never crossed that line.

Oh yeah. One more thing. I drank myself alcoholic. No history of trauma. No childhood neglect. No genetic flaw. If it could happen to me, it can happen to anyone.

If you are still drinking, and you are trying to find the will and the way to quit, the first step is to shed the shame. Sure, we do despicable things while drunk. Taking the steps to eliminate those atrocious behaviors is imperative. But dragging around the shackles of guilt won't make the challenge ahead any easier. In fact, we humans often drink to eliminate shame. If you are ashamed of your alcoholic label and your alcoholic behavior, you make the chances of defeating your affliction infinitely worse.

If you are in an alcoholic marriage with an active drinker, you can't make your spouse change. You can't make your spouse quit. It just doesn't work that way. But you can understand the origins of the predilection to your own considerable relief. If everything in your spouse's life pointed him toward an alcoholic destination, maybe you can trade-in some of your anger for compassion. It won't fix your relationship, but maybe it will bring you a shred of well-deserved peace.

If you are trying to save your marriage now that the alcohol is out of the way, leaving the wounds exposed, resentment is the greatest obstacle standing between you and reconciliation. Your road ahead will be daunting and require patience you probably don't think you have. You can make the journey a little easier by shedding the burden of blame and shame you carry for your spouse. It isn't your fault, nor is it your spouse's fault. Alcoholism is a disease. Hold yourself and your spouse accountable for the present and the future, but assign as much blame as possible for the damage of the past to society's cure for stress, sadness, boredom and anxiety. Blame won't fix your problems any more than sobriety will.

For some of us, probably most of us, alcoholism was our destiny from birth. We must pay the price and own the consequences, but we can't move on and put our disease in remission until we move past the stigma into a healing, healthy space.

You might forget who drove the Budweiser car at Indy in 1978. You might get confused and think Nancy Reagan's mantra was, "Show Us Your Tits!" You might forget the nickname my friend and I gave each other on a cold concrete floor at the University of Illinois. That's fine.

Those details aren't important. If you remember nothing else, please remember this: shame is no match for forgiveness.

chapter 2 | diabolical mind

I was a drinker for about 25 years, starting in the second half of my teen years and culminating with my last drink at age 43. For most of that time, I drank regularly or even daily. I consider the last 10 of those years to be the period when I crossed the invisible line from consistent, heavy drinking, into suffering from the disease of alcoholism.

Addiction is a self-diagnosis. There is no test you can take or physical examination with definitive results. That last decade marks the period from my first real attempt at long-term sobriety, until I made it over the hump into lasting recovery. I feel like that first true admission—to myself and my wife—that I was in trouble, changed my relationship with alcohol forever.

During my alcoholic decade, I had long stretches of sobriety, and also long relapses when I justified my drinking and tried to put rules around my consumption. My first attempt at sobriety was significant for two reasons: first, I had no idea what I was doing, and thus, no chance at success; and second, once I admitted to myself that my drinking was a serious problem, that thought never truly left my mind. The truth is ripe for denial, but it is impossible to shake. Somewhere in the deep, dark recesses of my mind, whether I was drinking or attempting sobriety, I knew alcohol would never willingly release its grip.

But I also knew something else during my decade of active alcoholism that was equally profound. I knew that alcohol made me feel better than anything else in the world.

The euphoria I felt when about halfway finished with my third India pale ale was unlike anything I've ever

experienced. It was hypnotic and transcendent, and I was
willing to chase that buzz just about anywhere it led.

The Power of Euphoria

This is really important. Alcohol affects different people in
different ways. My wife never understood my fixation with
drinking because alcohol simply doesn't hit her in all the best
tingly places like it does me. Even when drinking regularly
and heavily, Sheri described the experience as one with
advantages and disadvantages. Alcohol makes her feel tipsy,
not euphoric. The sense that she is inhibiting her own brain
function is there. For me, that feeling was undetectable.

For Sheri, on about her third drink, she can feel her body
and brain start to reach for the off switch. Even on occasions
when she would push through and party all night, she was
aware of a conscious decision to keep going despite
unavoidable negative consequences. For me, there was no off
switch, no warning light and no desire for anything but more
alcohol. The next day was always miserable for Sheri. Even
now, one or two glasses of wine, with their high sugar content,
gives her a headache the next day that makes drinking
regrettable. My hangovers were mild, unless I mixed tequila
with wine, beer, whiskey and ouzo, and drank it out of a
smelly cowboy boot.

I couldn't relate to Sheri's reluctance to drink, and she
couldn't relate to my fearless and relentless pursuit of the
euphoria. Do people who get bad hangovers and have to
push through the warnings and glaring off switches become
alcoholics? Absolutely. It happens. If there is enough trauma
they are trying to drown, or enough neglect that they don't
have the tools to function sober, people like my wife can

become alcoholics. There is no doubt about it. But that's not what happened to me. My alcoholism was a euphoric inevitability.

I only experienced one "slip" during my 10 years of active alcoholism. I'm defining a slip as a period of extended sobriety, that contained a one-time return to drinking, followed by more continued sobriety. What I mostly experienced was a lot of full and intentional relapses. I would be sober for a number of weeks or months, then talk myself into drinking again. And once I restarted my relationship with alcohol, I drank for weeks, months or years before admitting sobriety was again a necessity in my life.

This is important to understand, because it speaks to the long-term unsustainability of determination and willpower. Except for one time, I never slipped. Instead, I made conscious and well-thought-out decisions to try to drink again. Just as I had given every ounce of white-knuckle willpower to my periods of long-term sobriety—when I decided to drink again, I was just as determined to, "make it work this time." But it never did. Whether abstaining all together, or trying to control the uncontrollable, willpower is no match for alcohol.

On one such occasion when I stopped stopping, I have a vivid memory of giving myself a pep talk, and vowing to never quit drinking again (that's a lot of double negatives, and appropriate when applied to the discussion of the consumption of alcohol). It was summer, and I had been invited to play sand volleyball with a bunch of coworkers. This event combined all my favorite things: beautiful sunny weather, friends I loved, a smokey charcoal grill crackling with burgers and brats and icy-cold craft beers submerged in a huge cooler.

As I opened my third IPA of the afternoon, I was walking
back to the host's home from the communal volleyball court
in order to relieve my bladder. To this day, I have a vivid
memory of silently yelling at myself that I absolutely had to
find a way to make drinking work this time. The euphoria
was so profound at that moment, that keeping alcohol a
constant component in my life was of the highest priority. I
had to keep it under control. I had to follow my drinking
rules. I just had to. Coming off a period of extended sobriety,
I could not possibly go back to that austere and depressing
existence.

Nothing was as important as my love of alcohol. Nothing.

In all my years of battling alcohol, both as a drinker trying to
find elusive control, and in sobriety trying to find meaningful
recovery, I was never as determined about my relationship
with alcohol as I was in that moment on that sunny summer
day.

But it didn't work. I failed again. Not that day, but
eventually, I drank too much and made a mess of my life.
Again. I don't remember the specifics. I don't remember
how many months I drank that time around before admitting
defeat. I don't remember the incident that returned me to a
pledge of sobriety. I don't remember and it doesn't matter.

There are two points that this everlasting memory makes
painfully clear:

One, I am an alcoholic, due in large part to the euphoric
feeling I experienced early in every drinking episode. If you
cannot relate to this feeling, you might be an alcoholic for a
different reason. Millions of people know the euphoria that

nearly destroyed my life, and millions more succumb to the disease of alcoholism without experiencing this level of bliss.

If you are not an alcoholic, and you are trying to make sense of the disease that afflicts someone you love, you need to understand this feeling of ecstasy even if you've never experienced it yourself. Don't consider the person you love to be weak or deranged because they are in the euphoric clutches of alcohol. Consider yourself lucky because you're not.

And two, willpower is a fallacy. Determination is simply no match for the brain disease of addiction. I'll get into brain chemistry and the power of the subconscious mind later so you can better understand what's going on inside the skull of an alcoholic, but for now, please understand that none of us are as tough, strong, smart or in control as we think we are. Once our brain has associated alcohol with survival (and that's what the euphoria is all about), determination is like an annoying little gnat on a mule's ass.

Permanent sobriety requires a lot more than human effort. Permanent sobriety requires changing everything, from your patterns to your very identity. Alcoholism isn't about the weakness of lousy willpower, as it is popularly misconceived.

To remain high-functioning in the throes of addiction requires unimaginable strength. To beat the disease takes even more. Permanent sobriety requires not just strength, but the intelligence to embrace the fact that recovery comes from understanding the disease, finding connection with people who have been there before you, and seeking the resources that will allow you to change your life. Your whole life—not just the drinking part. Abstinence alone just doesn't work. I've got 10 years of stories about failure to prove it.

Chaotic Mind Syndrome

My brain needed a dimmer switch. When I was a drinker, thoughts bounced relentlessly around my gray matter. On far too many mornings to count, I awoke from restless nights of semi-sleep with a way-too-small number on my bedside clock, and my thoughts already racing at light speed. It was a combination of anxiety and paranoia, and the focus of my sporadic attention was as variable as a roll of the dice. Sometimes I was fixated on a problem from work. Other times, I was locked in on a parenting issue. More often than not, I started my mornings with thoughts swirling about my alcoholic overindulgence from a recent evening. It didn't matter the topic, really. My brain was almost always off and running before my feet hit the floor.

Alcoholism is a progressive disease, and this condition I call chaotic mind syndrome is a perfect example. I didn't always operate that way; my thoughts have not always raced out of control. The more committed I was to drinking, the more I lost control of my brain in my sober hours. The takeover was insidiously subtle. So subtle, in fact, that I didn't recognize a change was taking place. I woke up one morning with chaotic thoughts, and I just sort of assumed they had been there my whole life. It wasn't until I was over a year sober that the ricocheting synapses stopped firing. Only then could I look back and realize that alcohol was to blame for the chaos, and that it didn't exist before I started abusing alcohol.

The frequency of the bouncing thoughts was not the only thing that progressed diabolically. The mood of my thoughts deteriorated slowly over time, too. Constantly thinking is exhausting, but it's manageable as long as the thoughts are positive. It's when I began to be consumed by self-doubt, disappointment, unmet goals and a general sense of hopelessness, that chaotic mind syndrome transitioned from annoying to potentially deadly.

There were plenty of reasons for my change of attitude, and they were all alcohol related. Booze was causing conflict and anger in my marriage. Even an alcoholic can do the same things over and over with the same disappointing results, only for so long, before the insanity starts to take a toll. Likewise, my job performance was satisfactory, but not what it could have been if not shrouded in alcoholism. I was high functioning, so I did see moderate career success. I probably took two steps forward for every one I took back. Maybe the ratio wasn't actually that good, but I was making progress.

Still, those unnecessary steps back could not help but have an impact on my outlook. I also played soccer in an adult men's league, and I could never seem to reach my potential (even though my potential was pretty low) as a player. I was always too out of shape, too slow, with not enough accuracy with my touch on the ball. And I couldn't do a damn thing about any of it. My drinking wouldn't let me.

The consequences of the negativity were massive. My mood and outlook drooped, but the chaos in my head kept swirling. Eventually, not only was I relentlessly bombarded with thoughts, but the thoughts were of failure, mistakes and regrets. That was no way to live. In fact, it got so bad that there were times when I didn't want to get out of bed in the mornings. I never considered or attempted suicide. I had too many responsibilities and I loved my family too much to ever consider taking my own life, but I most certainly reached the point where I no longer wanted to live.

I have studied the lives and deaths of a lot of celebrities like Robin Williams, Anthony Bourdain, and Chris Farley. I firmly believe they had chaotic mind syndrome, too. They just had a much more severe case of it than I did. They were performers who felt safe and comfortable on stage or in front of the camera. That was their refuge. When the lights went down and the crowd went home, there was no applause and laughter left to drown out the swirling thoughts that hijacked their brains. Left alone to their own devices, that's when the darkness crept in. I'm familiar with the darkness. It consumed them, and it would have consumed me, too, if I hadn't spotted the tiniest glimmer of light and followed it out.

All of the men above, and countless other celebrities who have died of overdose or suicide, knew the same trick I know. When no audience is available to be entertained, when the cameras are packed away, and the stage is dark for the night, alcohol will make the chaos stop.

I am not a celebrity, so my natural comfort zone is not in front of an audience or a camera. Still, I was able to find peace from my chaotic mind when busy at work, when engaged in conversation with people I enjoyed, when playing or coaching soccer, or when enjoying some activities with my family. I could quiet the chaos. I could be in the moment.

But just as was the case with so many of the untimely celebrity deaths with which we are all familiar, I could also find peace from chaotic mind syndrome in a bottle. Alcohol could quiet the noise and make the self-doubt and regret simmer down for a while.

So many of us equate relaxation with drinking that we don't even realize relaxation becomes impossible without booze. We think we drink because we have found some free time and alcohol will enhance our enjoyment of it. The truth

is, for the millions who I believe suffer from chaotic mind
syndrome, the relaxation is not possible without alcohol.
Again, the booze is not an accessory, it is the main event.
Sitting still without a drink in my hand became an unbearable
exercise in self-loathing and trepidation about the future. So,
I didn't go there. I almost always had that drink in my hand,
and the alcohol convinced the chaos to cut me a break.

There are two problems with using alcohol to medicate
chaotic mind syndrome: the relief alcohol brings becomes
increasingly temporary; and alcohol is both the cure and the
cause of the condition.

We are all familiar with the concept of needing increasing
amounts of alcohol to achieve the same buzz. Similarly,
booze becomes gradually less effective at calming our swirling
thoughts. I never reached the point where I did not find relief
in alcohol, but the relief was fleeting and insufficient at the
end of my active alcoholism. Just like I would chase that two-
and-a-half beer buzz with more and more alcohol, I drank
increasing quantities or with increasing frequency to try to
keep the chaos at bay.

Alcoholism is said to be the disease of lies and deceit. In
addition, it is described as the disease of shame and blame.
But alcoholism is also the disease of more. Even with the
thousands of cases of alcoholism with which I have
familiarity, I've never heard of an incident where a person's
addiction made them want to drink less to achieve the
desired result. We alcoholics are driven to seek more and
more and more. Satisfaction becomes increasingly
temporary, and peace becomes elusive.

More, more and more just makes the chaos and
depression we are trying to treat with our beloved drink that
much worse. Alcohol is both the solution to, and the cause

of, all our problems. In no example is this truer than in the
case of chaotic mind syndrome. I drank to feel better, and
the alcohol made the pain come raging back stronger than
before. That's what makes chaotic mind syndrome deadly. At
the same time the booze is stopping the ever-swirling
thoughts of darkness, it also promises to bring them back—
darker than ever.

Alcoholism is a one-way street. If you don't like how you
feel, just drink more, and in the long-term, you can only feel
worse. Alcohol is the ultimate self-fulfilling prophecy of
destruction.

As my disease progressed, the arguments with my wife
became increasingly hopeless. My Monday morning
depression intensified and became more debilitating, joy
vanished from my life, and my self-esteem withered and died.

That's a lot of calamitous turmoil for a beverage I
welcomed into my life as a sign of adulthood and because of
the fun it promised. What a sucker I was. I'd feel worse if I
wasn't in such good company. At least I figured out the truth
before it killed me. Millions aren't so lucky.

Even Robin Williams couldn't make that funny.

Doritos Made Me an Alcoholic

No discussion about the factors that lead us innocently down
the dark and deadly path of alcoholism would be complete
without acknowledging all that we've learned in the last few
decades about how our brains work.

We'll explore the details of neurochemistry of addiction
in the second part of this book when we talk about recovery,
but for now, I'll explain how the hijacking of my brain didn't

start with my drinking. I paved the road to neurological addiction far before I started experimenting with alcohol.

I am a victim of the processed food generation. You are probably noticing how freely I assign the blame for all that ails me to society, and to the timing of my existence. That might seem like shirked responsibility and blaming others for my mistakes. Maybe, but if you get run over by a car when crossing the street, sometimes it's the driver's fault. I was just walking along, trying to stay out of trouble, and trouble hunted me down.

I own the wreckage of my marriage. I had to work harder to recover my relationship with my wife than on anything else in my life. I own my disease. Denying my truth didn't work. I know because I tried that for a decade. I had to face my addiction head-on in order to get my life back on track. But I refuse to blame my own natural deviance for my affliction. Ignoring the cause of this stigmatized disease is as dangerous as refusing to talk openly about the cure. I'm not excusing my behavior, but I am explaining it. I hope you can see the difference.

Starting in the 1950s, major food corporations began introducing convenience into our eating routines. By processing natural ingredients in new and innovative ways, these companies started selling tasty little food products complete with shelf stability, easy preparation and a lack of seasonality. To make these innovations even more enticing, these food miracles were affordable, too. By the time I was growing up in the 1980s, the food industry was perfecting their game and a huge percentage of the average American diet was comprised of convenience items.

We were too naive to consider the consequences of injecting our food with fillers, sugars and chemicals. The fillers made it cheap, the sugars made us crave more, and the chemicals meant we could leave crumbled bacon in a plastic shaker in our pantries indefinitely. We didn't know what monosodium glutamate was. It made our food easy, cheap and delicious, so we were fans...two forks up for progress!

Alcoholism has been around since the accidental inception of fermentation many centuries ago. But at the end of the 20th century, we introduced a new and more convenient way to prepare our unsuspecting selves for the ravages of addiction. You see, we learned quickly that the most popular of the heavily processed convenience foods were the ones with lots of added sugars or simple carbs that our bodies almost immediately converted into sugar. Sugar is highly addictive, so we became hooked. If you've paid attention to recent food trends and health warnings, you are probably already familiar with the dangers associated with the added sugars and simple carbs found in abundance in the processed foods that my generation couldn't seem to consume fast enough.

What you probably don't understand is that these sugars carved neural pathways in our brains preparing us for the eventual introduction of alcohol into our systems. Sugars and alcohol flow through our brains in virtually the same way. My neurotransmitters responsible for pleasure were warped by my daily after school Doritos fixation as a kid. When I started drinking a few years later, my brain already knew what to do with the alcohol, because it reacts just like sugar in our craniums. My highly processed diet doomed me before I even started drinking. Doritos made me an alcoholic. I never had a chance.

What a lame excuse, right? How can I blame my addiction on Frito-Lay? If my afternoon snack of chips and sugary soda was the only factor, I might have escaped unscathed and avoided my alcoholic destiny. But when you combine the unfortunate timing of my human adventure (growing up in the 1980s) with society's infatuation with all things alcohol, my family history of using booze as a pillar of adulthood and masculinity, the euphoric response I had to drinking, and the chaos of my overactive brain, the pieces of the puzzle all sort of fit together, don't they?

If you thought of alcoholism as a sign of weakness, I hope I've changed your mind. If you considered addiction to be an indication of depravity and moral deficiency, I hope you've reconsidered.

If you think the alcoholic in your life—whether that person is you or someone you love—is just a bad person, you suffer from the same lack of education about this disease that kept me locked in its clutches for a decade. It is not your fault. It is not your loved one's fault. I know that no one makes a person drink, but the free will argument just doesn't hold up when you consider all the forces working against us.

It is important to understand how we churn out so many alcoholics in this society, but even more important is understanding the cure. We'll get to that for sure.

For now, for your peace of mind and the start to the most necessary process of forgiveness, please release your grip on the blame. By doing so, you take a little power out of the stigma and move a step closer to your recovery from this diabolical and misunderstood disease.

chapter 3 | decade of demise

Think of your favorite annual event. It might be time spent with family or friends, it might be holiday related, or maybe it is an annual summer vacation. Or maybe it's a yearly getaway, just you and your spouse, or a huge party where there are a lot of people.

Whatever pops into your mind as your favorite day or week on the calendar, I bet there's booze there. Am I right? In fact, I bet the event is centered around alcohol, isn't it? Maybe not initially, maybe that's not how it was originally intended, but somehow, over years or decades, the drinking became the star of the show. At least it is for you, isn't it?

Or maybe you're not a drinker, or not a big drinker. Maybe the event I'm trying to conjure is the best day of the year for your loved one who is firmly in alcohol's grip. You can picture it, can't you? The excitement that surrounds that time of year is palpable for the person you love. And for you, it is probably terrorizing. You probably get a knot in your stomach just thinking about it, don't you?

Keep that event in mind while you read this story about my favorite alcohol-centric event of the year. Don't get fixated on the venue, this is not a book about auto racing. You don't have to care about IndyCars in order to relate. In fact, you don't even need to know what IndyCars are (and no, Dale Earnhardt is not my hero).

My Alcoholic Decade Begins

Everyone had a drink in their hand—every single adult at the party, except for me. I didn't know what to do. Should I just drink water or a can of soda, or was it less obvious if I didn't drink anything at all as I mingled with friends I had known my whole life? I was so frustrated! My mind fluctuated back and forth between the fixation on my indecision about drinking something non-alcoholic and feeling ridiculous for my incessant worry about such a non-issue.

But it wasn't a non-issue. It was a very big deal. Two weeks prior, I had finally had enough. I awoke full of regret and shame with a wife who was infuriated with me once again. It was the last time. I had admitted I had a problem with drinking, and I wasn't going to go through that anymore. I was determined. The two weeks had been full of temptation and doubt, but I had made it so far. What I faced that night, before the Indianapolis 500 in 2007, was an entirely different beast. Now I was surrounded by drinkers, and I had no idea what to do.

I admitted to my parents earlier in the day that I was not drinking anymore. We were at lunch after arriving in Indianapolis from our respective homes thousands of miles apart, and my drink order was conspicuous. I guess that should have been a sign that I was on the right path with this sobriety thing. So unbelievable was my decision not to drink beer with lunch that my parents asked me about it. I told them boldly that I had made a big decision, and alcohol was not going to be part of my life anymore. Their expressions painted a picture of knowing acknowledgement, betrayed by a hint of stunned skepticism. There was so much emotion in the glares they returned following my declaration, you'd think

we would have had a long, heartfelt talk about it. But we
didn't, because alcohol problems aren't things we talked
about in my family. Not back then. Not us. Not anybody,
really.

Everyone moved so easily through the Night-Before-the-
Race party. Could they sense my discomfort? Did they
wonder why I wasn't drinking? Were they all imagining me as
a raging alcoholic monster? Did they assume I had been
convicted of a DUI? Were they wondering if I'd destroyed
my marriage, especially since Sheri didn't make the trip this
year? Did they all talk about me when I excused myself to
use the bathroom?

The truth that eluded me that night was that no one cared
that I wasn't drinking. The host of the party offered me a
mixed drink since I had taken no interest in the wide
selection of beers and wines. "So, you're not drinking, huh,"
he said when I declined. I took a deep breath and prepared
myself for a series of probing questions. If he asked what was
wrong with me, I would tell him I just felt better when I
didn't drink. If he called me an alcoholic, I would shake my
head in confusion, and tell him I didn't know, but I didn't
want to find out. If he told me I was ruining his party, I would
slink away and go to bed early. I braced myself, as he opened
his mouth to speak. "Let me know if you change your mind,"
he said as he patted me on the shoulder and walked to the
door to greet some guests.

That was it. No one else asked. Humans are naturally
self-centered. That's not meant as an insult, but it is a very
telling fact. They didn't care what I drank or didn't drink, as
long as my abstinence didn't affect them. The alcohol was
flowing so their needs were met. My needs weren't of
concern to anyone.

When the party was over, I laid in bed and stared at the ceiling. I was relieved to be out of the torturous setting surrounded by drinkers drinking, but the shame from my pathetic existence lingered in the still of that night. Temptation to give in and join in the consumption had been mild at worst. Cravings for alcohol weren't the problem that had my eyes pinned open while everyone else got a couple of hours of sleep before the race. My insomnia was because I felt like a cretin—unable to drink because I couldn't stop once I started. I was weak. I was defective. I was a disgrace to my family. I didn't want to go to the race in the morning. I wanted to crawl in a hole and die.

I didn't drink that Indy 500 weekend in 2007. I made it through the race gritting my teeth and feeling like the only person among the 300,000 spectators who didn't get all tuned up. I made it back home holding onto my sobriety by my fingernails. Within a week of returning to Denver, I started drinking again. It wasn't a matter of willpower. I didn't succumb to a trigger. I just didn't want to live my life as the degenerate who couldn't partake in the reward of adulthood. I would have to try harder to get a grip on my drinking. I would have to make a plan and exert more energy. I just had to find a way to control the uncontrollable.

That was the first of many times that my sincere and hopeful attempts at sobriety failed because of the shame and stigma associated with alcoholism. I tucked the memory of that race weekend away in the dark corner of my mind where I stored bad ideas and concerns exaggerated. I had no idea at the time that I had just kicked off the most painful and despicable decade of my life.

The Rules

Every single alcoholic I know (and I know thousands of them) went down fighting. I've never met anyone who, at the first signs of danger, put down their glass and walked away. We all try to hold on to our relationship with our beloved drink.

In an effort to control the uncontrollable, we put rules around our drinking. We recognize that once we start drinking our ability to reason is severely impaired. Our only hope of maintaining some degree of composure is to set predefined limits we hope our feeble little human minds can follow. We can't, but that doesn't stop us from trying.

Here are the rules I tried to follow for the last 10 years of my drinking:

Only drink on the weekends. This rule is popular in the heavy-drinking community because it is temporarily, occasionally successful. My adult men's league soccer games were Thursday nights, and my teammates and I always celebrated, win, lose or no result, with pints in the pub attached to the arena. Because of the convenient timing of these games, I defined the weekends generously as Thursday nights through Sundays. This meant I had excruciating Mondays, Tuesdays and Wednesdays. Often, I stayed sober for those 72 nail-biting hours. Sometimes the stress, depression, temptation, anxiety, cravings or exhaustion got the best of me and I drank on the weekdays.

The truth is, if the wind blew just right, it was enough to tip me over the edge and abandon this rule. Even when I was successful, I was miserable waiting on the edge of my seat for

Thursday night to roll around. Drunk or anxious, I wasn't much fun to be with.

Liquor is off limits. Probably the most common tactic adopted by struggling drinkers is to swear off the hard stuff and vow to only drink beer or wine. I tried this for most of the 10 years of my active alcoholism. I was able to hold to my self-inflicted restrictions for the most part. So how did I compensate? I drank really strong beer, and lots of it. Occasionally, I would just get sick of beer and wine, and indulge in whiskey or vodka. But usually that happened after drinking a ton of beer, so as you can imagine, the results were never pretty. To this day, it is mind boggling to me that I once thought the solution to my drinking problem was to limit myself to an unlimited quantity of 7% ABV beer.

Counting drinks. When sticking to beer was astoundingly unsuccessful, I tried to limit my consumption. This was another long-standing rule onto which I hung a lot of hope. I had set amounts of beer I allowed myself in specific situations on specific days. For example, I tried to limit myself to two IPAs on weekday evenings. I wanted to chew my own arm off when I finished the second beer every night.

This rule makes as much sense, looking back, as going to a strip club. Why would I want to get all jazzed up and excited only to slam on the brakes with no satisfaction? Two beers were nothing more than a tease for me. On regular, boring, stay-at-home weekends, I limited myself to a six-pack of IPAs. On big weekends that involved parties, dinners or other festive occasions, my limit was 12. That's right, I considered drinking half a case of strong beer all by myself to be a success if I didn't get into the other half. Thinking about it now, I can't believe I took pride in sticking to this rule. If you are where I was, you probably think this limit sounds reasonable.

It's five o'clock somewhere. Growing up in my family, the drinking started at noon on weekends. Therefore, I never understood 5 p.m. as an appropriate marker to pop the cork. Drinking in the morning, however, was always off limits for me. There were exceptions, of course. We drank mimosas on Christmas. Sometimes we tailgated for football games in the morning. Brunch isn't brunch without a Bloody Mary. You were probably anticipating this one, but the Indy 500 drinking started as soon as we were upright from the night before. In my neighborhood (I bet yours, too), four-year-old's birthday parties on a Saturday morning include a cooler of beer for the dads. The list is endless really, so I'll end it here, because I think you get the picture.

Water between drinks. This is one of my favorite rules for its apparent logic, and because it is completely ludicrous. In this ridiculous plan, I drank a full, 12-ounce glass of water between every alcoholic drink. The concept was that it both slowed and diluted my consumption. The truth was, I spent most of most nights really drunk swaying in front of a urinal. This one didn't work even a little bit.

Never drink alone. This one got expensive, quickly. I was constantly making excuses to meet friends out for drinks. This one was a short-lived disaster.

Light beer only. This is one of my favorites for overall destruction of both my health and wallet. For a short period, I allowed myself unlimited beer, but it had to be low alcohol (like 4% ABV) light beer. The idea was that light beer was mostly water. It just made me feel like a hillbilly surrounded by crushed cans of Coors Light. This was one of my wife's favorites, too, because the gluttonous chugging enhanced her growing disdain for me and my growing beer belly. Believe it or not, I was willing to exert the extra effort it took to get drunk.

At the end of my decade of addiction, I employed a combination of those first three rules. I only drank beer (no booze), I tried to abstain Mondays-through-Wednesdays, and I kept to a specific beer count. Guess what. Not only was I often unsuccessful at adhering to those rules, but even when I did, they didn't solve any of my problems.

I try to stick to telling my story, and it either resonates or it doesn't. This approach keeps me out of fights. You might not like what I have to say, but you can't argue with the events and emotions of my life. Disagreement is not an option—I'm not talking about you; I'm telling my story full of my experiences and my failures.

But there are a few aspects of alcohol abuse that have transcended in my mind, based on the stories of so many others, into cold, hard, indisputable facts. Here's one that can save you years of agony, but only if you are in a mental and emotional position to listen:

If you've started putting rules around your drinking in an effort to exert control, you've crossed the invisible line into addiction, and there is no going back. Sobriety is your only chance at a peaceful and happy life.

That's harsh, I know. I sound like an arrogant asshole. I know that, too. You can spit and claw and scoff and argue all you want. That, my friend, is a fact of a drinking life, and there is no way to get around it.

If you are trying to control your drinking with rules, you have three options:

1. Stop drinking now, get help, find recovery and save your life.
2. Stop drinking later after wasting another huge chunk of your life because you think you can do the impossible. You risk total destruction.
3. Drink yourself to death.

But what do I know, right? I'm just a degenerate alcoholic who likes to write his depressing stories with a little flare. I'm not a PhD or even a certified [something]ologist. Why should you believe me?

I told you how my decade of alcoholism started. Now I'm going to share the details of the 10 years that followed. If you don't believe me because of the thousands of cases of addiction to alcoholism I've studied, maybe you'll believe me because of the pain I endured, and pain I inflicted on my family.

If you think you're stronger than I was, or better or more determined, please keep reading. If the drinker you love refuses to address the issue, please brace yourself for a glimpse into your future. This isn't about my arrogance. The three options explained above aren't facts because I have an insecure need to be correct. I wish I was wrong. I wish your destiny wasn't so defined.

How do I know I'm right? Because if I wasn't, I'd still be drinking today.

Controlling the Uncontrollable: A Decade of Relapse

I'm not sure how many times I stopped drinking and subsequently relapsed, between the Indianapolis 500 of 2007, and the start of my permanent sobriety in January of 2017. I made at least half a dozen attempts to quit drinking over that period, probably more like eight or ten tries.

Each time I tried and failed, I learned something important. I talk a lot about building sobriety muscles. When we first quit drinking alcohol, we are remarkably weak. Our resolve is insignificant against both the temptation to drink, and our subconscious mind that wants to follow the patterns we've spent years grooving. Each relapse is a chance to learn something about ourselves and our disease, and build those sobriety muscles a little stronger for the next attempt to get over the hump.

But each time I tried and failed, I also made my relationship with my wife significantly worse. Resentments build on both sides of an alcoholic marriage. I got drunk, said things I should not have, did things I'd later regret, and sulked around ignoring my beloved family. My wife reacted to my intoxication and verbal abuse—and said and did reprehensible things herself. In each case of my overconsumption, we added bricks to the wall of resentment between us. When I failed at attempts at long-term sobriety, that failure added great vertical spans to the wall. I might have learned each time I tried, but I also made reconciliation that much more impossible.

Looking back, I wish I'd had access to the lessons of others. Maybe that would have shaved years from my alcoholic sentence. Maybe I could have learned how to better

manage the situations that caused me to relapse time and
time again.

Maybe if I had understood the pitfalls, I would have been
able to avoid them.

I was alcohol. My early attempts at sobriety were thwarted
by the persona I had built starting with my alcohol
experimentation in high school. The more I drank, the more
I enjoyed drinking and being around drinkers, the more I
looked forward to drinking in the evenings and weekends,
the more alcohol became a significant part of who I was.

Eventually, I didn't just drink because I liked how it made
me feel, I drank because I liked the message it sent to
everyone around me. I was a drinker, and damn proud of it.

Do you remember the billboard with tough and rugged
pictures of the Marlboro Man with a cigarette dangling from
his lips as he stared invincibly into the distance? I never
understood those ads because I was raised believing cigarettes
were bad for me. Even when I smoked in college, I knew it
was a mistake, and I knew I would quit in order to save
myself from a certain death from cancer. Those
advertisements never worked on me, but they killed millions
in the generations that came before. The ads said that
smoking wasn't about flavor or a mild buzz, it was about
being an attractive, tough, independent man.

I didn't buy what the Marlboro Man was selling (I didn't
buy the image, I did buy the product), but I bought into the
same embodiment of classy, joyful and glorious adulthood
from alcohol. And it was an easy sell, because I didn't need a
billboard for examples. The adults of my childhood made
the sale. So, when I was considering sobriety, it wasn't just
about physical and psychological cravings. I had to reconsider

my whole persona. I was a drinker. Without alcohol, who the fuck was I going to be?

If you're not a drinker, when I talk about suffering through sobriety at a party full of drinkers, full of shame, self-hatred and disconnection, it probably makes no sense. But to us drinkers, the stain of abstinence glows bright like a scarlet letter of weakness and evil. This cannot be overstated. My very identity as a drinker kept causing me to relapse from periods of sobriety lasting as much as six months on several occasions.

When I read the memoirs of alcoholics in recovery who came before me, I found that this was the part they left out. Drinking, destruction, more drinking, more pain, then: recovery. I often read about working the steps and finding a sponsor. I read about fighting temptation and dissolved relationships. But I almost never read about the drinker carving out a chunk of his soul and living through the experience until a healthy chunk grew back to replace it. That's what it was like for me. If I wasn't going to be "Matt the drinker" anymore, I had to patiently wait to figure out who this new me would be.

I quit drinking for you. At other times, my attempts at sobriety failed because I quit drinking for the wrong reason. A therapist friend of mine taught me an important lesson about human behavior. He explained that there is only one reason people make significant changes in their lives. A person can only change when the pain of not changing becomes personally unbearable. It's not about the pain they are inflicting on others. That kind of pain is grueling but is not enough to cause a change in the perpetrator's behavior. Only when we cripple ourselves will we successfully adopt new behaviors.

I wish I had understood this lesson on the several occasions when I quit drinking for my wife, because Sheri asked me to quit, or because the pain I was causing her filled me with regret. It sounded like such a noble cause. "I quit drinking for you, Sheri!" I screamed on more than one occasion when my sobriety didn't fix our problems. I tried. Hard. I really wanted sobriety because I knew she wanted, even needed, for me to get sober. I wish I had been successful. Now I know that was not possible, and I wish I had known my gesture had absolutely no chance at success.

Sobriety doesn't work that way.

Because my impetus for abstinence was beyond the human realm for successful personal change, I failed. Every single time I quit drinking for my wife, I relapsed with traumatic consequences.

Had I just kept drinking, Sheri's disgust would have continued to build, but I would not have cracked open the door of hope. By declaring my resolve, then faltering, I made matters in my relationship much worse. Each time I chose to start drinking again, I chose alcohol over my wife. Second place is not a sustainable position in a marriage. The line that separated Sheri's hatred of alcohol from her feelings about me grew more and more invisible with every relapse. Sure, I built my sobriety muscles through lessons learned each time I tried to recover from my addiction, but my failed attempts did far more harm than good.

Same life, drink-free. I was determined to prevent sobriety from affecting my life. Knowing what I know now, that statement is the definition of lunacy. On several attempts at long-term sobriety, I decided to go about my normal life, just without a drink in my hand. On one such occasion, my neighbor invited me to a Colorado Rockies baseball game with him and his friends when I was a couple of weeks into sobriety. "Not only will I go to the game with you," I yelled back over the fence, "but I'll be your designated driver!" What a mistake. I watched as my neighbor and his friends attempted to drink their faces off.

It was a complete shit-show and one of the most challenging nights of my life. I stayed sober that evening, but I was drinking again within a week. Rather than avoid temptation and otherwise unpleasant situations in early sobriety, I was determined to not let my sobriety influence my decisions. Back when I was drinking, I would have taken great pleasure in getting hammered with my neighbor and his friends. So, in my warped logic, I had to accept the ballgame invitation because that's what my active alcoholic self would have done. I put myself in so many miserable situations thinking that way, and even when I survived, the shame and pressure proved too much in the days that followed. Relapse was inevitable, each and every time.

NA aficionado. To avoid the shame of no longer being a drinker, I once decided to become a non-alcoholic beer connoisseur. This one is harder to explain because it defies logic. I think the idea was that if I could no longer consume alcohol, I would transfer my expertise from IPA to other types of lagers and ales, but the zero ABV kind. Nope, even with that second sentence, I still don't understand. Needless to say, it didn't work. I started drinking the real stuff after a few weeks of skunky, impotent golden-amber drizzle.

Look away! There's nothing to see here. I tried faking it, too. I ordered soda water with a lime and ice in a nine-ounce rocks glass with a tiny plastic stir straw, and pretended it was gin and tonic. I ordered non-alcoholic beer and poured it in a glass, so it looked like the real deal. I carried an empty beer bottle around a party secretly filling it from the bathroom sink from time to time. The problem with all this deception was that it did nothing to cure me of my resistance to change. I was still the guy who was a drinker from head to toe, now I was just deceiving everyone around me. Stuff like that was okay for short-term, white knuckle situations in early sobriety, but it was no way to go through the rest of my life. It was not well thought-out; it was doomed to fail from the beginning.

I am hopeful you can learn from my lessons of a decade of failed attempts at permanent sobriety. If you are a drinker in trouble, please let my experiences help you build your sobriety muscles. Your story is not exactly the same as my story, but I'm confident your results could be indistinguishably similar if you learn these lessons from me, rather than the brutally hard way.

If you are the loved one of someone who needs to quit drinking, let my story be a warning for your life ahead. Sobriety doesn't fix anything. It only exposes the wounds that alcoholism leaves behind. If you can convince the one you love to get help now before the wounds of resentment grow incurably deep, your relationship might have a chance at peaceful redemption.

A decade is a long time. For me, 10 years was wasted, wasted. My kids grew up during that decade, and my wife and I grew apart. It doesn't have to be that way for you. Use my example to build a better future for yourself. You don't have to experience a rock-bottom moment in order to justify your sobriety. You don't have to waste any more of your life trying to control the uncontrollable or breathing hope into a hopeless situation. It doesn't have to end in a violent explosion and burn to the ground in a flash of flames.

Whether you are a troubled drinker, or you love someone who is, your bottom is when you stop digging and start climbing.

chapter 4 | love and alcoholism can't coexist

I stepped onto the balcony of our third-floor apartment in St. Paul. I needed a cigarette. Sheri and I had been arguing again, and it was best for me to cool down. The Minnesota winter would surely do the trick. As I leaned over the railing, sipping my rum and Coke, I heard the lock snap down on the sliding glass door behind me. I didn't bother to turn around. I knew what happened. The love of my life locked me out again...literally and emotionally.

A few hours earlier, I had arrived home from work shortly after Sheri, and I poured my first drink before I even took my tie off. The anticipation of the relief only alcohol could bring started building shortly after lunch. I made it to that day's finish line, and nothing would deny me my reward.

I also poured that first drink before giving my future bride more than a cursory nod and a smile. As I felt the rum warming its way down my throat, I turned to hug the woman I loved. My message was received. Even before we were married, Sheri was the second most important thing in my life.

The evening had a predictable progression from there. It's funny how even as my actions set the stage, and even after so many similar tension-filled nights between the two of us, I could never see it coming. Alcohol occupied my attention, numbed my intuition, stunted my subtlety and suffocated my charm all at the same time. Soon after we arrived home from work, we were arguing about nothing in particular.

Blinded by my Love of the Drink

The popular societal definition of insanity is doing the same things over and over again, yet expecting different results. Alcoholism is often described as a version of insanity. My relationship with my wife certainly did nothing to dispute that assertion.

We drank (sometimes just me, but often both of us on the weekends), got into meaningless arguments over insensitive comments or unimportant disagreements, fought like our very survival depended on victory over our life partner, and fumed for hours, or even days sometimes. At the worst of times, we spent entire nights locked in battle, while I continued to refuel along the way, of course.

There was no room for compassion or understanding. The alcohol squeezed that right out of us. My intoxicated mind was fixated on the black and the white of every issue, with no perception of any sort of gray area. Once wounded by my refusal to compromise, barbed assertions and insults, Sheri unleashed her pain back on me. She could give as good as she got, leaving us locked in relentless, circular battles.

Don't misunderstand. I'm not blaming Sheri for her retaliation, vicious as it could be at times. The blame for our constant disagreements lies squarely on my shoulders, and on the demon in the bottle that I welcomed into our lives. Sheri was simply defending herself, and she learned through painful experience that the best defense was offense.

Looking back, the part that defies rational explanation is that I could never make the connection between the alcohol and our inability to get along. I loved Sheri, and she loved me, but whenever we were together, the potential for conflict was ever present. The only other two things that were consistently around when our tempers boiled over were booze and our cat, and Baghera wasn't fessing up to starting anything.

The cycle continued for years, even decades, as we got married, had four kids and built a business and a life together. Something about the disconnect between alcohol and the arguments kept hope alive in me that we'd figure it out and stop fighting. I suggested we treat each other better, and practice patience and tolerance whenever tensions rose. I analyzed the arguments trying to pinpoint the spot where civility turned sour, and our love was replaced by aggression. How did it happen? Who was to blame? What could have been done or said differently? Why couldn't we just get along? I wanted to know, but I refused to look at the obvious intoxicating culprit.

I never gave up. I searched and searched for the reason our love wasn't enough to avoid conflict. It had to have a logical solution, and I was determined to find it. We both had tempers. We were both stubborn people. I offered suggestions for behavioral changes for both of us, not understanding how impossible it is to change those around us. I kept digging and clawing for the answers, and I often drank while performing my exhaustive analysis.

For Sheri's part, she went along with my pursuit of understanding about the conflict between us. She listened to my explanations and suggestions, but all the while, the truth gnawed at her relentlessly. "Why do you have to drink every day?" she would ask. It felt to me like she was trying to pick a fight. To Sheri, she was moving closer to the elusive answer.

As the pattern stayed the same for me—drink, argue, stew, blame, forgive and move on—the situation slowly and insidiously deteriorated for my bride. Where I maintained hope that we would figure it out and the relationship would improve, Sheri's feelings for me took a serious blow each time the cycle repeated. For her, hope had long since faded, and her questions were about just how bad it would get.

This point is important. My love and affection for Sheri remained constant through the many years of disagreements. Sure, I wanted to fix our problems, but the arguments did not impact my feelings for my wife. For Sheri, it was a different situation. She could see, even when she couldn't verbalize it, that the conflict emanated from alcohol. My love affair with beer and booze not only left her feeling like the second most important thing in my life, but it also enhanced her hopelessness that our situation would ever improve. Her pain and skepticism were a serious blow to her feelings for me.

We both hated the arguments, yet, while the love I felt for Sheri was unwavering, my bride slowly fell out of love with me.

This distinction cannot be overlooked. I am not claiming to be better or more devoted than Sheri. Quite to the contrary. I find it tremendously insightful that my ignorance or denial as to the role alcohol played in our relationship kept me moving forward unwaveringly. At the same time, Sheri's perception of the damage alcohol was doing changed her feelings for me.

I didn't know where to assign blame, so I didn't. Sheri knew my drinking was tearing us apart and she couldn't ignore the truth. Every time I chose alcohol over our marriage, it made her love me a little less.

Many marriages adapt and survive active alcoholism. That's what happened to Sheri and me. While I kept trudging along through our tumultuous marriage, ignoring the truth and unable to make changes, Sheri's coping mechanism was quite different. She put her love of our kids in front of everything. Even as my drinking was the cause of all our problems, I was still a pretty good father, and Sheri wanted stability for her children. She knew our business and our home were reliant on our ability to hold our marriage together, so she stayed.

As the years rolled by, and the resentments from the arguments mounted, her love for me faded. Despite her feelings, she didn't leave. She stayed for the things that became higher priorities in her life than I was. Sheri adapted. Our marriage adapted.

Unconditional Love

As devastating as my addiction was, Sheri was determined to protect her children, and the marriage to a man she no longer loved.

I couldn't sense the changes taking place in her. I remained oblivious. Through it all, the toll of destruction mounted. I grew quite adept at pushing down the pain and moving on.

On one particularly vicious night of alcohol-fueled fighting, I tore our bedroom apart. I ripped off the bedding and threw books and pictures around the room. I pulled the permanently attached mirror off the vanity, and I yanked the chimes off the antique doorbell built into the hallway. We both yelled and screamed, and we both feared the escalation of my out of control behavior. Sheri consoled Joey, a toddler at the time, and the only one of our four children who didn't sleep through my eruption of rage.

That incident left a mark on Sheri and our marriage, but not on me. It took a few days, but eventually, I was ready to put the episode in the past and move on. Sheri, however, added the terrorizing experience to the growing wall of resentment that prevented her from trusting me.

Another time, Sheri and I fought all night before leaving for a family vacation the following morning. I continued to drink as we argued and was still quite drunk when I got behind the wheel to drive my precious family to the airport. We spat and whisper-screamed insults back and forth on the 35-minute drive. We tried to keep our disagreement from affecting the kids, but neither of us could access rational discretion that horrible morning. At one point on the drive, I yanked the steering wheel to the left, squealing the tires as I turned the car around heading back toward home. When I abruptly changed my mind and decided to continue to the Denver International Airport, again, the tires screamed as I jerked the car in the opposite direction.

My alcoholic actions left all six of us shaken and destroyed our hopes for a peaceful, relaxing vacation. It left a scar on the older kids and is seared in both my memory and that of my beloved wife. That was among the very worst days of my life, and I still carry relentless shame for my behavior in endangering everyone I loved the most that day.

As for Sheri, that morning on the way to the airport changed the way she felt about me forever. When I say that sobriety doesn't fix anything, incidents like that explain exactly what I mean. No amount of sobriety could ever ease Sheri's hatred for the danger I created and terror I inflicted on her babies that day. She has forgiven, but she'll never forget. And our relationship will never fully heal. That scar will be there forever.

These are two of the worst experiences of our alcoholic marriage, and two of the most traumatic days of our lives. For

the most part, we kept the destruction away from our
children. Mostly, we did not fight in front of them. We were
careful not to wake them when we argued in the middle of
the night. Neither of us lost sight of how innocent and
vulnerable they were, and we both remained vigilant to
protect them. Mostly.

But kids are so very intuitive. They are listening even
when they pretend they are not. Even when they reject the
lessons we try to teach them, our love and good intentions
can't help but get through to them. Likewise, when we don't
think they notice our bad behavior, they usually do. They can
sense tension the way a predatory animal can sense fear. Our
kids could pick up what we were laying down, even when we
did so quietly.

Sunday nights marked not just the end of the weekend
but the end of my drinking-fests, as I tried to follow my rules
about not drinking on weekdays. Therefore, my mood was
sullen at best as the work week loomed. I would sulk around
the house and drink in isolation in the basement. During the
day on Sundays, I would have sports on the TV and look like
most American dads drinking beer and watching the game.
But as evening rolled around and the athletic contests were
done for the weekend, I'd keep drinking and drinking as I
flipped channels and oozed an aura of pathetic-ness.

The dichotomy was thick with irony. As I sulked and
drank away my stress and anxiety in the basement, setting a
depressing and repulsive example of selfish gluttony for our
children, Sheri would spend hours lovingly preparing a
homemade Sunday night dinner. I don't think she
consciously counteracted the stain left by my awfulness, but
the result was indisputable. Sheri dedicated her Sunday

afternoons to creating a loving and nurturing example for our kids while I wasted away.

I rarely screamed at our children. I almost never turned my drunken anger into punishments undeserved. But still, my disease took a toll on our kids. They learned to not ask for things once they saw a drink in my hand. They felt the unspoken rule about keeping their rambunctious noise levels under control once I started drinking. I had a good relationship with my kids even when alcohol dominated my life. But I didn't have a great relationship with them. I didn't nurture them as much as I wish I had. I wasn't the dad they deserved.

My subtle, but undeniable parenting neglect had a massive impact on my relationship with my wife. Sheri's unconditional love for her children resulted in a disdain for my selfish lethargy. As if our marriage could withstand further attack, my alcoholic inadequacy as a parent drove yet another wedge between us. And because I didn't abuse the kids, neither verbally nor physically, I thought everything was fine. So what if I sulked away my Sunday afternoons, I thought. I'm an adult, and I deserve some time to unwind. I was blind to the impact I was having on my innocent protégés. But Sheri wasn't blind, and what she saw sent a dagger straight through her heart.

So much damage done, and not all of it was emotional. Alcoholism has the power of complete destruction, and it crushed the physical bond of the love between me and my wife, too.

Drowning Intimacy

Intimacy is such an important component of a healthy marriage. When Sheri and I first started dating, we couldn't keep our hands off each other. We were young and ignorant about creating an intimate bond of love, but we didn't let that stop us from trying. Our sex life was full of abundance and eagerness, and the alcohol only made things easier. Shyness, caution and inhibitions melted away as we drank before almost every interaction of young, physical love.

As time passed, the role of alcohol in our intimate lives morphed from a welcomed enhancement to a growing barrier between us. The connection between physical attraction and emotional comfort is strong in Sheri. As we argued and resentment grew between us, her eagerness for intimacy suffered severely. She just didn't want to be with me anymore, and pleasure for Sheri was drained from our physical relationship, no matter how hard we both tried to restore it in the moment.

Partly out of a sense of marital duty, partly to avoid additional arguments, and partly because she did still partially love me, Sheri did not decline my advances. The frequency of our sexual activity remained high, even as the satisfaction became completely one-sided. Sheri gave her body to me, even though she was capable of accepting nothing in return.

When intimacy dies in a marriage, it can happen in one of two ways. Either the physical contact ceases, leaving both partners painfully aware of the existence of serious problems between them, or the sex continues in a loveless and robotic fashion. In some ways, it is more damaging to continue to be physical when the interaction is devoid of intimacy, and that's exactly what happened to us.

Not only was Sheri uninterested and resentful of our sexual activity, but I became unfulfilled by her lack of interest. So emotionally painful was our physical interaction because of the lack of passion or pleasure, that we would have been better off to avoid contact. "Fine. I guess so," was a far more painful answer than, "No," would have been. Sheri's heart was so empty that it began to drain the physical love from me, too. She was doing what she thought was best. She was continuing to perform physically even as she was emotionally unable.

Even then, when we added loveless sex to a relationship full of fights, disagreements and sulking depression—even then, I could not see the connection between alcohol and the demise of my marriage. In fact, the case was quite the opposite. Because our sexual relationship started when we both drank heavily, I was convinced Sheri would loosen up if only she would drink with me. So many weekend nights ended in disappointment as I pestered her to drink while we watched a movie or had dinner, hoping it would lead to excitement in bed later.

I was begging Sheri to partake in the same elixir she most despised for the impact it was having on our relationship, and the slow destruction it was wreaking on her husband. Booze was killing me. Alcohol was killing us, and yet I was urging her to adopt my diabolical habit.

Looking back, it is hard to believe how much obvious damage I ignored in the interest of keeping my predilection alive. It defies logic and is hard to understand, let alone explain.

Think about all the devastation to my marriage at the hands of alcohol for a minute. First, the alcohol-induced disagreements made our life together unbearable. Then, the impact my drinking had on our kids, even though it was most often indirect, it made me even more unattractive and unbearable to my wife. And last, as the attraction evaporated, our intimacy was completely eliminated, leaving in its place sexual engagement that left far more hurt and loneliness than the momentary relief and pleasure it provided. Booze was responsible for every single aspect of the deterioration of our marriage. And I couldn't see any of it. None.

Alcoholism is widely considered a disease of deceit and denial, and the lies we tell ourselves are among the most diabolical and painful. I refused to see the negative impact alcohol was having on my life. Admitting that truth would have forced me to face the demon far earlier than I was otherwise ready.

You see, there was a ranking system in the part of my brain that I couldn't access on a conscious level. Alcohol had a firm grasp as the top priority in my rankings, and anything that threatened to replace booze was denied access. The truth and honesty about the damage I did to my marriage is so obvious and glaring now—but was simply beyond my reach when it was taking place. My alcoholic brain protected itself from the truth. Despite all the evidence, I considered alcohol to be innocent of all such charges.

This point is important no matter which way alcohol addiction impacts your life. If you are a drinker in trouble, you can't possibly imagine how much damage your abusive drinking has done and continues to do. That information will not be available to you until months or years into your long-term sobriety, and there are no shortcuts. This isn't about taking inventory or making amends. This is about not being able to see the forest through the trees.

If you are in early sobriety, you are on a slow and painful path of discovery. For you, this isn't about self-hatred and beating yourself up. The damage is done, and your continued recovery depends on your self-forgiveness and self-love. At the same time, however, you must understand the depth of the hole you dug when drinking and acknowledge the resentment that piled up against you. The process is slow and deliberate, and we'll address it in the following two parts of the book. For now, the key is to understand that your behavior when drinking caused problems your alcoholic mind wouldn't allow you to comprehend. You will comprehend it now in recovery, and your ability to do so with repentance and grace will determine so much of your future.

If you love someone who has let alcohol cause unspeakable damage in your life, may you find some consolation in the understanding that the person you love simply doesn't mean to cause you pain. I'm not making excuses, but I am providing an explanation. Have you ever wondered why the person you love can't see the damage and pain? Emotional blindness is a real and deadly side effect of alcoholism. I'm not asking you to forgive. That's up to you. I'm only trying to provide you some comfort in understanding that the pain inflicted is not intentional, and it carries with it a lasting burden of grief and remorse.

Relationships are as rewarding as they are challenging. That we use alcohol to make them easier, and think we are going to get away with it, is one of the great mysteries of human existence. We have to stop lubricating discomfort and lowering inhibitions in the interest of getting to know each other more easily. Making life partners isn't supposed to be easy, so why do we look for shortcuts in a bottle, at our own long-term demise? Maybe if we have trouble connecting with someone when we are both sober, that's not the person to whom we should dedicate our future. Alcohol is just a tool we use to defeat our impatient nature. But nature wins in the end, every damn time.

If you know the pain of an alcoholic marriage, I hope you'll keep reading. The road to salvation is long and extremely difficult, but we made it, and maybe you can, too. It all starts with understanding, and that's what I hope you have found in our painful story. Just like sobriety doesn't fix anything, but it is a prerequisite to recovery, understanding doesn't guarantee love.

But love is impossible without it.

chapter 5 | selfish pain

Even now after years of sobriety, the ceiling fan over our bed stirs the most terrifying of memories. I can't tell you how many mornings I woke, hours before dawn, gripped with anxiety and debilitating depression from the alcohol I consumed the night before, and stared at that ceiling fan. It was as though the answers I so desperately sought could be found in its rotation. Sometimes now, when I lie peacefully in bed, especially when I have something on my mind and I can't quite seem to shut my brain down, the blades of that fan yank me back to the trauma of my alcoholic past.

Every time I awoke in panic about my drinking, my whole body was damp with sweat. It was a combination of toxins oozing from my pores, and stress perspiration brought on by my complete and total inability to fix the problem that had hijacked my life. My pulse was quick, my breathing shallow and my mind raced to find the elusive answer. The thing I wanted the most was to gain control of my drinking, yet, the only thing I seemed totally incapable of doing was controlling my drinking. I was stuck.

My situation was getting worse. There was a consistent increase in the severity of the anxiety and depression. At first, my middle-of-the-night wake ups were jarring and uncomfortable, but I managed to move past them with relative ease. By the end of my active alcoholism, I lacked the physical strength and mental desire to get out of bed. I was never suicidal, thanks to my love for my kids who depended on me, but I most certainly wanted to die. I prayed God would take the pain away even if that meant He had to take my life.

I'm not telling you about the depth of my pain and despair to gain your pity or for the purpose of literary drama. The degree to which I was out of options, suffering immensely and quite literally nearing death, is extremely pertinent because it is the reason I found the strength to stop drinking alcohol.

Do you remember in a previous chapter when I explained that there is only one reason humans make significant, fundamental changes to our behavior patterns? Do you remember that reason?

Pain.

Not pain inflicted on others, but pain we endure ourselves. And the pain required for me to remove the most important thing in my life, from my life, was massive and unavoidable. There is a myriad of reasons why I became an alcoholic, from family history to societal influence to the euphoria I felt. I even share the blame for my affliction with Doritos. But there is only one reason I quit drinking alcohol. I was in unbearable pain.

I exhausted all the options. I tried every rule I could imagine to control my drinking. My wife and I worked on our relationship and attempted various changes to our personal behaviors to find ways to get along and reverse the direction our marriage was heading. I prayed to God ceaselessly asking for the solutions to my problems. I found alternative outlets for stress like exercise and spiritual activities. None of it worked. None of it even slowed the progression of the disease that would surely have eventually killed me. The pain grew in frequency and severity until I could endure it no longer.

My story does not include a crash-and-burn, wake-up call kind of bottom, but I definitely had a bottom. My own rock bottom came the morning I woke up to the realization that my choices were only limited to:

1. Stop drinking alcohol; or
2. Die.

I had spent a decade trying alternatives to these two choices. They were all unsuccessful, and I crossed them all off my list of options. It was over. My failure was complete.

Pain Inflicted is not Enough

During my 10 years of active alcoholism, I was not the only one trying to solve my addiction problem. My parents asked my Methodist minister to lead an intervention (much to my considerable disgust for exposing the family secret). He refused, stating his opinion that interventions don't work. The necessary component missing in any intervention, he told my parents, was a desire by the alcoholic to quit drinking. It is not enough, he went on to explain, for the rest of the family to want it. Very insightful and totally true, I now realize.

At one point on our miserable journey together, my wife presented me with an ultimatum. She demanded that I quit drinking, or she would leave and take the kids. The thought of losing my children was terrifying, and it did make the decision to quit easy. But it didn't last. I remained sober for some time, then gradually reintroduced alcohol in a slow and measured way. For a while, I held it together. By the time my drinking was once again out of control, Sheri's threat had passed, and our cycle of disagreements and temporary reconciliations continued.

I think sometimes about what would have happened had she left. Would I have stopped drinking and attempted to win her back, or would I have drowned my shame from my failed marriage, and transitioned from a high-functioning alcoholic to something much worse?

Sheri still feels shame for what she considers a lack of strength to hold firm and leave me after she drew the line in the sand. I don't see it that way. I think her intuition won. I think that deep down she believed in me. I also think she knew that eventually I would find permanent sobriety, and we could begin to work on our relationship. I believe Sheri's love for her children was stronger than the hopelessness she felt about our marriage. I believe she stayed for them.

This is such a difficult component of our story, and the story of every alcoholic marriage. To stay or to leave—what a terrible predicament for anyone to ever have to face. There is no universally right or wrong answer. Small nuances in the situations we face in relationships embroiled in addiction make major differences.

I have only one piece of advice to offer to anyone who faces such a heart-wrenching decision. You must protect yourself and your children first. You are of no use to the alcoholic you love unless you are safe and can cling to your emotional and physical health. Anything that stands in the way of your safety, or that of your children, needs to be removed from the equation. Even if that means turning your back on someone you love. Even if you have to watch your spouse self-destruct from a distance.

Here's the bottom line: you can't save the alcoholic you love.

One of the most devastating parts of my alcoholism for me was coming to the realization that my actions caused my wife, and occasionally my kids, pain. When I woke at 3 a.m. and stared hopelessly at the ceiling fan, my thoughts were often of the vile things I said or did to my beloved wife. But as much as I hated myself for the pain I inflicted on her, it wasn't enough to make me quit drinking.

If you love someone who abuses alcohol, I believe there is only one thing you can do to help, and only if you don't put yourself at physical or emotional risk in doing so. You can help your drinker understand how dire their own personal situation truly is. You can explain the progressive nature of the disease. You can point to the pain that the drinker you love is personally experiencing. If living without you or your children has become necessary, and you are confident you can hold the line once you draw it, then explain the pain of loss and loneliness that your drinker is going to endure.

» Interventions usually don't work.
» Ultimatums are risky, and often end in the opposite of the desired result.
» Pain felt by others is tragic, but it doesn't bring about sobriety.

You can show the way, but ultimately, the alcoholic has to be in enough selfish pain. It's the only way.

Ineffective Alternatives

The "Sober Curious" movement has a lot of momentum, and for some drinkers, it is having significant benefits. The idea is that you don't have to consider yourself to be an alcoholic in order to find a better life without alcohol. I believe problematic drinking is on a spectrum. On the one end, you have an occasional, light drinker who doesn't experience euphoria from the glass of wine or two consumed once or twice a month. On the other end of the spectrum is the end-stage alcoholic who is on the doorstep of drinking himself to death. The rest of us are somewhere in between.

There is no doubt in my mind that I crossed the invisible line that separates consistent drinking from alcoholism. My disease was spiraling progressively, and there was no going back. Exactly where was I on the spectrum? In the middle? Toward the end-stage? I don't know the answer, and frankly, I don't care. For me, sobriety was not a curiosity, it was a life-saving requirement.

The danger the "Sober Curious" movement poses for people like me is significant. I needed to quit drinking. It wasn't about wanting to try something different. For people in my area on the spectrum, wherever that is, the idea of experimenting with sobriety to see what happens is potentially deadly.

Here's the real danger: we high-functioning alcoholics present to society like drinkers who might have a curiosity about sobriety. Because we give no outward signs of the debacle drinking has become internally, we consider cutely named experiments like "Dry January" or "Sober October" to be viable options. They are not. This isn't a game.

The promoters of 30-day, 90-day or one-year sobriety experiments are well-intentioned. The idea is that the benefits of a period of abstinence will be so profound that the drinker won't want to drink again. I get it. For some people on the spectrum, I suppose it makes logical sense. But for drinkers like me, no amount of good intentions makes up for giving us a glimmer of hope that the period of sobriety will "reset" our drinking back to normal. That's just not how it works.

I don't think there is an alcoholic in long-term sobriety that didn't try to learn to be a moderate drinker before committing to the very austere and restrictive decision to abstain completely. There is no such thing as learning moderation for an alcoholic. This isn't about willpower or mental weakness; this is a matter of brain chemistry. Once our brains associate alcohol with survival, the lesson cannot be unlearned. In permanent sobriety, we can put the lesson in remission and return to a totally normal existence—but as soon as we reintroduce alcohol to our systems, our brains remember.

Robin Williams was sober for 20 years before he decided he could drink alcohol again. Many times I have watched his interview with David Letterman conducted shortly before his death from suicide. Williams explained that when he decided to start drinking again, after two decades of sobriety, it took until the second or third day before he was in a more severe alcoholic condition than when he quit all those years prior. Two or three days, that was it. And there are literally millions of examples of this same experience.

Do you know what I have never heard of? A case where a prolonged period of sobriety reset a person's brain so they could control alcohol again. It is a farce. It doesn't exist. Teaching people to control alcohol is a phrase often used to sell books and online programs. I should know, I bought a number of them looking for a more reasonable option than sobriety. I hope my example, Robin Williams' example, and the experiences of millions of others, can save those who come after us some time, frustration and pain.

Now, with the expanding legalization of marijuana comes another troubling trend. An increasing number of people are willingly trading addictions. Smoking weed often results in a mellow, lethargic reaction from the user. This contrasts favorably with the angry or aggressive reaction many people experience when they drink alcohol. So, there is a sizable trend whereby people switch to smoking marijuana from drinking alcohol because their behavior is less offensive to the people around them.

Chill, hungry zombie is an upgrade from loud, destructive asshole. I get it.

But here's the thing: just as sobriety doesn't fix anything in a relationship, switching from one addictive drug to another won't ease our internal pain. Marijuana hijacks the pleasure center of our brain and distorts neurotransmitter function just like alcohol. Weed is not a solution to alcohol. Marijuana can only enhance and prolong the damage we initiate with booze. This is exactly like putting lipstick on a pig.

Look, I'm not the smartest guy in the world, but I'm not an idiot, either. As for persistence and tenacity, I've got a larger-than-average allotment. If there was a solution to alcoholism that didn't involve permanent sobriety, I would have found it. I searched relentlessly for 10 years. You can transfer your problems, hide your problems or deny your problems. But if you want to solve your problems, it is time to get serious. It is time to get and stay sober.

Unexpected Enlightenment

Looking back, I believe it was a miracle that I found sobriety when I did. There was so much about this diabolical disease I had not yet learned. I did not understand the indisputably progressive nature of addiction. I didn't know that if I felt totally hopeless one day, I would feel even more hopeless after the next time I drank too much. In active addiction, I never fully grasped how tenuous my fingernail hold on my high-functioning life really was. I was so close to losing it all: my family, my house, my career, my finances, my reputation and my freedom. The denial inherent in every alcoholic prevented me from seeing how near I tread to the edge of disaster.

There is something else I did not understand about permanent sobriety when I made the decision to quit drinking. I lacked the capacity to understand what a blessing my freedom from poison would eventually be. I'm not talking about the rainbows and unicorns professed on social media. I never experienced waking up every day thankful to be alive and filled with joy. I'm talking about something deeper and far more meaningful than any of that.

The profound benefits in permanent sobriety that I continue to experience now took years to discover. The word, "recovery," does not do it justice. For me, my whole world opened up and I found life-changing enlightenment in my dedication to sobriety. Some of the benefits were revealed after a year. My second year was even better than that, and the way I felt after three years of sobriety was nothing short of transcendent. And the discoveries continue today.

I've reached a point where I cannot imagine drinking alcohol for any reason. If God Himself stood next to me and promised no ramifications if I decided to drink again, I wouldn't do it. Nothing could make me trade this level of peace and enlightenment for the lies in a bottle I chased for 25 long years.

It is hard for me to believe that I had no idea how my life would transform, and yet I still found the strength to quit drinking. That speaks to the power of intense pain. It is the only power strong enough to bring about the changes required to beat addiction to alcohol.

Are you ready? Are you in enough pain? Is the person you love suffering enough to remove the poison from your relationship? Is it time to stop digging and start climbing?

The road to enlightenment is long and treacherous, and the correct path to take is often uncertain and full of unexpected challenges. In the next two sections, I'll share everything I know to help you find freedom.

The first step is clear. There is no ambiguity, and there are no options. I'm ready if you are. Take that first step. Relieve your pain in the only sustainable way.

Stop drinking. Keep reading.

evolving into sobriety

Part Two

chapter 6 | alcoholic monster

Alcoholism is the disease of deceit and denial. Everyone knows that. I will make no attempt to dispute that fact—all my experiences confirm it. But just like our society mistakenly attributes addiction to weakness and a lack of willpower, we also believe the lies of alcoholism are inherently evil. That's the kind of misguided assumption that gives the stigma associated with alcoholism all its strength.

The morning after a night of heavy drinking was always like putting together a jigsaw puzzle for me. Did I say things I should regret? Did I keep it within reason, or did I drink way too much? Did I anger my wife? Or did Sheri get frustrated and cold, and did she anger me? By some miracle, did I make it peacefully to bed at a reasonable time, or did I bake a pizza pan full of cheesy nachos at 2 a.m. and spill most of it on the kitchen floor? The morning after was so often a mystery.

As I pieced things together, I usually became contrite and apologetic. But other times, I became angry at my wife's intolerance for my need to let loose and enjoy my weekend downtime. On those occasions, I often wasted an entire Sunday trying to help Sheri understand what she should do in the future to be less of a flaming, insensitive bitch.

When I decided, on the mornings after, that I went too far, drank too much and all disruptions from the night before were my fault, I spent that next day convincing myself that if I tried harder, I could keep it under control the next time. On the mornings after when I was certain Sheri's intolerance was to blame, I spent that next day trying to convince both of us that she just needed to be a better person. In either event, it was a day full of lies and denials.

The Family Secret

That's the deceit of my alcoholism. In order to keep believing that my heavy drinking was normal for a hard-working professional family man, I had to convince myself that alcohol was not to blame for my problems. My lies were never intended to hurt anyone, and they were anything but evil. I was lying to protect my predilection. Denial was the only way to keep my love affair with alcohol alive.

On a few occasions, when I felt particularly ill-equipped to handle the realities of the day, I mixed vodka with my coffee and carried my travel cup into our church sanctuary to medicate my way through a Sunday morning sermon. There were times when I secretly took slugs of whiskey straight from the bottle in between the beers I was publicly consuming. At my parents' house in South Carolina, we have to walk past the enormous liquor cabinet with dozens and dozens of exotic bottles when we go from the outside to the kitchen.

On many festive vacation occasions, I stopped and secretly sampled as I made that journey throughout the family fun-filled days. Sometimes when entertaining guests at our house and drinking many beers with all the guys in attendance, I would retreat to the kitchen to open another bottle of wine for the women, and chug as much as I could before returning to the party to refill their glasses.

On each and every one of those occasions, my clandestine drinking was necessary to ease the panic that I would not be able to publicly drink enough. I needed those extra drinks. I deserved to feel the relief that only my excesses could deliver. Again, there was nothing evil about my intentions. My deceit was all about chasing the euphoria and trying to keep my demons at bay.

I didn't lie about having an extra-marital affair. I didn't leave the house every morning pretending to go to a job I had lost due to my love of booze. I never denied consuming alcohol when I had been drinking, although I often underreported the quantity consumed; both to my wife and to myself. I never pretended to have car trouble or problems at work so I could go to the bar and blow off my responsibilities.

I was a high-functioning alcoholic. My belief that my drinking wasn't a problem was dependent on my belief that I wasn't doing anything wrong. Had I stopped believing my own lies, had my deceit become egregious and punitive, I would have lost my own belief that everything was okay. And me believing that everything was fine was the foundation on which I continued to drink.

I'm not trying to convince you that I was a good guy even when I was a drinker. Defending my reputation is not at all the point. Understanding that the lies of alcoholism are an unavoidable symptom—a sort of collateral damage that is equally innocent and bitterly painful, to us drinkers and the people we love—is vital to your recovery.

If you are a drinker who needs to stop drinking, the shame of your disease will hinder your progress in recovery. If you love someone who drinks, denies and lies, your misperception that their deceit is malicious will make their recovery almost impossible, keeping you locked in a cycle of anger and hatred. If you are trying to recover your relationship now that you have removed alcohol from the equation, this message might be most important to you. There is so much pain involved in an alcoholic marriage. Thinking of your partner as evil, because of the lies and denials of alcohol addiction, will make reconciliation unachievable.

I'm not asking you to forgive unconditionally. I had to work through my deceit in order to move forward and be able to stand myself in sobriety. Likewise, we had to deal with years of resentment before my wife could begin to heal. Forgiveness requires both acceptance of reality, and sorrow.

I am asking you to understand the repercussions of the disease of alcoholism.

The stigma associated with alcoholism defines the alcoholic as an evil liar, determined to destroy lives with weak and selfish intent. That's just not how it works. Until we understand the truth, and speak about it openly and honestly, we'll never defeat the stigma. If the stigma remains strong, alcoholism wins.

You are a Victim

A person who gets cancer is universally viewed as a victim, every single time. Even if the patient smoked two packs of cigarettes a day for 50 years before receiving a diagnosis of lung cancer, that person is a victim. We might scoff at his ignorance or poor decision making, but we will still drive him to treatment, cook and deliver meals, pray for his whole family and sit by his bedside holding his hand and providing comfort. The same is true for people who battle obesity, diabetes and heart disease. They are all victims. Even though lifestyle choices carrying known consequences are the most significant factors in all our most deadly diseases, we still rightly consider those sufferers to be victims.

What about alcoholism? In our society, the drinker is considered to be a selfish deviant with a lack of willpower. He spends his whole life immersed in advertisement and cultural influence that encourages alcohol consumption as necessary for celebration, mourning, stress relief and estimable adulthood. We practically pour the booze down his throat. Then, when he gets the disease that results from his most desirable lifestyle choices, do we consider him a victim? Absolutely not. We shake our heads and whisper about the damage he wreaks on his family and about how he wastes his life.

» No meals are delivered.
» No rides to treatment are offered.
» No hand holding or bedside sitting is considered.
» And the prayers are for those the alcoholic monster has harmed, and for him to get his head out of his ass.

One of my best friends lost her mother to cancer. That was the official cause of death, and that's what my friend and her family told everyone. When I confided in my friend about my alcoholism, she shared with me the truth about her mother. Her mom had a very treatable form of cancer, but her liver was far too damaged for her to survive chemotherapy, so she died because the lifesaving treatment wasn't an option. My friend's mom drank enough to render her liver useless when she most needed it. My friend's mother died of alcoholism.

Almost no one knows the truth, because cancer is a
socially acceptable cause of death, but alcoholism is not.
Alcoholism is a disease of denial and deceit all right, but we
alcoholics aren't the only ones telling the lies.

Do you want to cure alcoholism? Then cure society's
misperception of the disease and the epidemic will be over.

Alcoholism has many victims, and it all starts with the
alcoholic. If you drink alcohol and develop an addiction, you
are a victim of a deadly brain disease. It is not cancer or
diabetes or heart disease. It is worse. Alcoholism is
statistically just a little bit more prevalent than these other
chronic diseases, and just like those, it is extremely deadly.

Recognizing the alcoholic as a victim of alcoholism is a
cornerstone of successful recovery. The word, "victim,"
lessens the shame and eliminates the blame for contracting
the disease. I want to be extremely clear as I make this point.
As alcoholics, we must take responsibility for our actions. If
we have legal issues, financial collapse or if our disease has
destroyed our relationships, it is our responsibility to deal
with those consequences. I am in no way suggesting that a
diagnosis of addiction is an excuse to shirk our
responsibilities and walk away. Before we can move on, we
have to pick up the pieces.

Here's the point, though: we should not blame alcoholics
for becoming addicted to one of the world's most highly
addictive substances, one that is ever present in our lives.
There should be no shame. Alcoholism isn't a "them"
problem. It is an "us" problem. It strikes the young and the
old, the poor and the rich, the beautiful and the faces only a
mamma could love, the skinny and the fat without concern
for race, gender or sexual orientation. That we suddenly

transition people from inclusivity to outcast, because
alcohol's undertow gets ahold of them, is a travesty.

First generation, or with a family history going back
centuries; smart enough to know better, or full of innocence
and ignorance; stubborn and confident, or easily influenced
with low self-esteem—none of it matters. If you are an
alcoholic, you are a victim. Lose the shame associated with
your diagnosis. It will only make the challenge of recovery
significantly more daunting.

If you love an alcoholic, you are a victim, too. All the
careless, cruel and demeaning things I said to my wife landed
right in her heart. All the times I tried to shift the blame away
from the alcohol and onto her intolerance or moodiness,
Sheri was left confused and ashamed. And when she stayed
with me knowing no human deserved the treatment she was
enduring, she suffered in hopeless silence. She is the most
obvious victim of my disease.

So are all the loved ones of all of us alcoholics. I'm not
going to waste a lot of words convincing you of one of the
indisputable truths universally accepted about the disease of
addiction. The people who get close to the fire are the first to
get burned. In a society where we lack compassion for
alcoholics, we can all empathize and sympathize with the
people who love them.

If you love an alcoholic, your voice needs to be heard.
One of the most significant tragedies in the stigmatized and
silent way we ignore alcoholism, is that the stories of the pain
and endurance of the people who love us alcoholics are
rarely spoken out loud. This needs to change, but it is a bit
tricky. The purpose of telling the stories is not to bring shame
and embarrassment to the alcoholic, it is to bring respect and
admiration for the people who keep loving us.

My wife has been through painful and emotionally crushing experiences as the spouse of an alcoholic. Her strength should be revered. When she protected our children from the volatile repercussions of my excessive drinking, she deserved our respect and admiration. When she endured my sulking, alcohol-induced depression and sexual neediness, her mental strength and reliance on her faith was a testament to her character and resolve. When she kept showing up, day after alcoholic day, and worked and prayed for a better tomorrow, she was an inspiration for all such victims who come after her.

But the story of her strength is never told. Only the story of my weakness, with a side order of pity for my spouse, finds its way into the light of day.

We are looking at it all wrong, and our blindness is deafening. We need to hear the stories of courage and resilience in the name of hope and love. We need to celebrate the heroes who survive alcoholism as the second-hand drinkers. If we are going to defeat this disease and eliminate the stigma, the power of the loved ones who persevere will have to be the headline.

As long as we ignore the disease in silence, instead of treating it with full-throated admiration for those with the courage to keep fighting against the odds, the stigma will survive for generations to come.

We are the victims—all of us. The drinkers, those who love us, and the people who will never have the opportunity to learn from our shameful, unspoken mistakes. I'm not asking you to pity us, but I do hope you'll pray for us and love us.

I'm Not Sorry, I'm Not Ashamed

All chronic diseases impose burdens on the afflicted and the ones they love. Have you ever spent significant time with people battling cancer, heart disease, obesity or diabetes? There are dietary restrictions that have to be adhered to, treatment can be painful and time consuming, all of these conditions zap the energy levels of the victims, getting around can be slow and tiring, and the love we feel for those burdened by the disease is emotionally taxing and worrisome.

Yet, I've never heard a cancer expert recommend to someone fighting for her life that she needs to make a list of all the people her disease is impacting and apologize to them. I'm not aware of an amends process for heart attack victims. Taking inventory of people burdened is not, as far as I know, a part of the treatment for diabetes or obesity.

Why not? Why don't we recommend to the victims of chronic diseases that they apologize to the people who love them? Because it would immerse the process in shame, that's why. And shame is counterproductive to the recovery from illness. Shame has no place in the treatment plan of any disease. Not even alcoholism.

I am directly responsible for the survival of my wife and my four kids. Likewise, my wife carries the same responsibility for me and our children. We are a unit functioning together for our mutual benefit. Therefore, because of this vital responsibility I carry for these most important people in my life, I feel like I owe them the very best of me.

I am very sorry for the pain my disease has caused my wife and kids. I have apologized many times, and my sorrow and repentance will continue until the day I die. They depended on me, and at times, I let them down. I will never fully forgive myself for the impact my alcoholism had on their precious lives.

But for me, that's where the amends process ends. I see no benefit in groveling for forgiveness from other humans for the impact my disease had on them. I was no more of a burden than a person diagnosed with any chronic and potentially deadly disease.

My parents worried. I wish they had not suffered so, but it was not my fault. I am not sorry, and I am not ashamed. My sister was afraid. It sickens me to think of her in distress, but it was not my fault. I am not sorry, and I am not ashamed.

At times, I was boorish, arrogant and slobbery as a drunk. The people around me endured my obnoxious behavior. I wish I had kept it in control, but it was not my fault. I am not sorry, and I am not ashamed.

As I said before, we alcoholics must own the consequences of our actions, drunk or not. I did not cause a financial disaster for my family because of my drinking, but we surely would have a lot more money had I not guzzled down so much of it. I own that. I've been blessed to spend a lot of time with my kids as they grew up, but I also wasted a lot of time being wasted. I could have been a better father. I own that. I've done immeasurable damage to my marriage because of my alcoholism. My disease is not my fault, but I take responsibility for the repair of my most connected and intimate relationship. I own that, too.

Ownership of responsibility is very different from suffering the shame of the collateral damage of our disease. One of those things is an admirable trait to which we should all aspire. The other is cloaked in guilt, humiliation and stigma, and has no place in pulling lives from the wreckage of alcoholism. If we want to get clean, we should spend as little time as possible wallowing with the pigs in the mud.

None of this is easy. I would never suggest that changing a lifelong perception about a disease we are too ashamed to talk about is a simple task. It is not. Viewing alcoholism as a disease, and alcoholics as victims, might not be a comfortable place for you to go. Here's the thing though: a blame and shame mentality won't get you where you deserve to be. Just as sobriety doesn't fix anything in a marriage, stigmatized humiliation won't get any alcoholics sober. And without sobriety, none of us stand a chance.

Alcoholics are victims of a brain disease. This statement doesn't really jibe with the traditional beliefs of alcoholism as a spiritual deficiency, or a sign of deviant weakness. But neuroscience is proving that our traditional beliefs about alcoholism are narrow-minded and obsolete. It is time to adopt this new statement. If you don't believe alcoholics are victims of a brain disease, nothing else in this book is likely to help you recover from alcoholism or save your marriage. I hope you are open to new ideas and a different perspective, because our traditional approach has a dismal success rate. Blame and shame aren't curing anyone.

In order to heal your mind, you might just have to change your mind.

chapter 7 | popular misperception

For most of the 10 years that I suffered as an active alcoholic, I played indoor soccer in an adult men's league. The games were on Thursday nights, and when we finished playing, my teammates and I got an early start to the weekend by heading to the bar to celebrate victory or soothe the sting of defeat. On one of my many attempts at sobriety during my decade of addiction, I told my teammates I would not be joining them in the bar after our game. I was about two weeks sober, and I wasn't feeling strong enough to drink water while watching them drink beer and get louder as they repeated themselves; all behaviors that eluded my detection when I, too, was drinking.

Guys often bowed out of the postgame camaraderie for various reasons like family responsibilities or prior engagements. I didn't think it would be a big deal as I explained I had to get home to help my wife with something.

As I turned to leave, one of my teammates yelled a question to me. This particular friend was an ordained Christian minister. He had a doctoral degree from a highly respected seminary, and he cared lovingly for his devoted congregation. In addition to preaching, he spent hours each week in pastoral care. As a trained clergical therapist, he counseled his flock as they dealt with a wide range of issues, certainly including substance abuse and addiction.

As I left the soccer arena that night, this highly trained, experienced and greatly respected friend of mine for many years called out, "Hey Matt! Where are you going? Do you have to run off to an AA meeting?"

All my teammates laughed. I was crushed.

I stood speechless for a few seconds, looking back at my friends over my shoulder. I managed a halfhearted grin and looked down at my feet as I walked to my car. I was extremely angry at my friend. How could he do that to me? I was so raw, so vulnerable and so weak. Despite his training and experience, he was completely ignorant to the painful difficulty of early sobriety. He was ignorant, society was ignorant and I was completely unprepared for the challenges I faced.

I didn't drink that night, but within a couple of weeks, the shame of not drinking was too much for me to overcome, and I returned to active alcoholism.

Public Misperception

The only positive I could latch onto at the time from the joke made at my expense by my friend, and the subsequent laughter of my teammates, was that it reinforced my determination to never go to Alcoholics Anonymous for any reason, ever. Under no circumstances would I join a group that was so publicly ridiculed and stigmatized. For me, because of my perception shared by just about everyone I knew, AA was not even a last resort. It was no option at all.

Alcoholics Anonymous supporters call their gathering places, "the rooms," and I had a picture ingrained in my mind of cold metal folding chairs in a damp church basement. I envisioned the saddest, weakest, most depraved among us chain-smoking cigarettes, eating stale doughnuts, drinking bad coffee and whining to each other about their lot in life. I wasn't one of them. I might have been an alcoholic, but I was nothing like the despicable inhabitants of those rooms.

That's what I thought. Because that's what four-plus decades of life in our society taught me, reinforcing the message time after time, through cinematic depictions and stories of hopeless relapse. If AA was my only option—and I very much believed AA was my only option—there was no solution for my condition. Ask for help? Not me. No way. Because I knew the response to my request, and I would rather have died than go there.

Does my opinion sound aloof, ignorant, and arrogant to you? It certainly sounds that way to me now, looking back. I'll readily admit that there is a certain selfish arrogance involved in alcoholism, but my complete rejection of AA was much less about my belief that I was strong enough to get sober on my own, and far more about believing the things about the organization that I had always been told.

Alcoholics Anonymous has a major public perception problem—and it's killing people. People like me who refuse to get help because of their perception of the inhabitants of, and environments in, the rooms. And the solution is not forthcoming as I am aware of no effort by the organization to work on public relations. The decentralized lack of structure of AA works in many ways. It has worked for them for almost a century since *The Big Book of Alcoholics Anonymous* was first published in 1939. But with the lack of a headquarters or hierarchy of decision makers comes a lack of ability to affect the labels and stigmas assigned to AA by society.

Alcoholics Anonymous is simply not in a position to effectively defend their own reputation, so the misperception continues. I'm hardly an ambassador for the organization, as my questions about its methodology extend far beyond the

questionable reputation, but I'll certainly do my part to set
the record straight.

Alcoholics Anonymous has saved millions of lives in the
past 80-plus years. No other organization, method, idea,
suggestion, philosophy or treatment has even a fraction of the
overall success of AA. The organization deserves to be
exalted as an international treasure for the good work done in
the addiction and mental health fields decade after decade
after decade.

And the perception I had, the same perception shared by
so many who have no experience with AA, one of folding
chairs and cigarettes and sadness—nothing could be further
from the truth. The rooms of Alcoholics Anonymous are a
place of hope, love, shared experience and compassion.

There is a certain magic to the connected healing that
takes place in the rooms, and some of my best friends in
recovery would likely be dead if not for the fellowship that I
so feared in the ignorance of my active addiction. I can think
of no other organization with whom I have no association
that has had such a blessed impact on my life by saving the
lives of so many people I love.

If you want or need to stop drinking, but you are having
trouble making it happen, I hope you'll consider Alcoholics
Anonymous to be a viable option. Don't fall into the trap of
my arrogance and ignorance. Check AA out. Don't just go to
one meeting. Go to a few meetings and meet as many people
as you can. Give it a try and really make an effort. Alcoholics
Anonymous is not for everyone, and I'll go through the issues
I still have with the organization, now speaking from a
position of having done the research. But it is the right
solution for many.

As they say in AA, you can use the parts of the program you like and leave the rest. Some people find great comfort in the fellowship. Others feel the steps are transformational if worked properly. Others still are all in, and live and breathe all the slogans and philosophies. You won't know what you think until you've given AA a serious chance. If it is time for you to stop drinking, I hope you'll do just that.

On the other hand, if you love someone with a drinking problem, I hope you don't view Alcoholics Anonymous as some sort of silver bullet, because it is not. As I have said, AA is a true lifesaver for many. But for many others, AA is not a good fit. I am painfully aware that many loved ones of people suffering from alcoholism have, with disastrous consequences, included mandatory compliance with AA as a part of their ultimatum to stay together. We all need to find our way to sobriety. If the path was easy, or even direct and consistent, there would be a lot fewer of us struggling to find freedom.

I have seen studies that report the success rate of Alcoholics Anonymous in the single digit percentage. I don't know that to be accurate, and I have read lots of comments from AA constituents disputing this failure rate, but the fact remains that many fewer people find success in AA than those who fail to sustain sobriety through the fellowship. That is much less of a condemnation of the program than it is a nod to the diabolical and confounding nature of this disease. Sobriety is the hardest thing many people will ever attempt, and AA is not the answer for everyone. That last sentence is indisputable by anyone with an open mind and experience in the field of addiction.

One of the dogmas of AA that I find most irritating is, "It works if you work it!" That puts the onus of success on the work effort of the afflicted. I know a ton of hardworking, committed people for whom the 12-Steps were not a solution. In fact, I fall into that category. The idea that Alcoholics Anonymous is the only answer, and the sufferer's dedication to the program is the only difference between success and failure, is both arrogant and ignorant. AA is an option. It is a good option with decades of history and millions of believers. It is not, however, the only way, no matter how absolute the mantra sounds.

AA Is an Incomplete Answer

The Alcoholics Anonymous doctrine views addiction as a spiritual problem. In 1939, the science of addiction was limited at best. We had no understanding of neurotransmitter function or the power of the subconscious mind. Our brains remain the final frontier of biology, and I am constantly reading tweaks on what we believe to be neurologically true, including new information that disputes the cranial assertions of just a few years ago. The causes and cures for alcoholism continue to evolve, and in the middle of the last century, the spiritual explanation was the only one that passed the smell test.

"Let go and let God," is another of the tenets of AA that I struggle to reconcile. My rejection of the doctrine has nothing to do with my own personal spirituality. I am a Christian with a strong belief in God. I just don't believe he wants us to hand him all our problems. I believe the purpose for our existence here on Earth is to see what amount of the human condition we can figure out how to manage for ourselves, in community with each other.

I'll never forget the afternoon I was jumpstarting the dead battery on my wife's vehicle with my Jeep. After connecting the cables, and while I waited for my wife's battery to charge, I prayed to God for the answers to my questions about my drinking. They were the same prayers I had mentally pleaded for God to answer so many times: Please give me the strength to control my drinking! Please tell me what to do to keep this under control! The requests were the same as always, but this time was different. This time, God answered.

As I stood between the front bumpers of our two Jeeps, I knew exactly what I needed to do. I needed to quit drinking. I could feel it. Control was elusive because I was trying to control that which, for me, was uncontrollable. God wasn't about to solve that problem for me, but I do believe he pointed me toward the only ultimate answer. I had to quit. There was no other way.

I didn't quit drinking that day. In fact, permanent sobriety was still a year or more in my future. But the sensation I felt was so profound that I'll never forget that mundane task with such divine repercussions.

I've had a strong sense of spirituality my whole life. Except for my college years, when I couldn't be bothered to get out of bed before noon on Sundays, I've attended church consistently. I have always prayed to God. I am not a kneel-down-beside-my-bed-and-fold-my-hands-while-I-bow-my-head kind of prayer. I just have a running dialog going with God a lot of the time. A preacher once told me that there is no perfect time or way to pray, and I solidly adopted that philosophy.

So, when I asked God for help controlling my alcohol consumption, the request was nothing new. I was also unsurprised to feel him throw the ball back in my court.

You're going to have to quit drinking, there, chucklehead. There'll be no moderation for you! That's what I heard Him say. There was no offer to take my problems off my hands. It was not suggested that I let go of my troubles and God would carry my burden. He suggested that I shift the task at hand from failed moderation to abstinence, but He never offered to do the work for me.

Here's the point: It is inconceivable for me to find a spiritual answer to a neurological problem, especially when I have been spiritual all my life. Finding God was not a solution available to me. I already knew God, we were buds. We talked all the time. Okay, mostly I talked, but occasionally I found the answers He put in my path. At no time has He suggested life would be easy. I do take great comfort in my relationship with God, and my heavenly destiny once my mortal existence is over, but I still have to do my imperfect, human best while I'm orbiting the sun. Let go and let God? That doesn't work for me.

Here's the other point: my spirituality is irrelevant when it comes to your sobriety, or the sobriety of someone you love. I believe in God. I believe sharing what I've learned about this wretched disease is my divine mission. But I don't in any way believe God is holding back freedom only for Christians. I believe He loves us all whether we love Him back or not. I believe the peace, freedom and hope that I have found in permanent sobriety is available to you regardless of your spiritual beliefs. I do believe our souls long for a spiritual connection, and those who don't have one have a harder time dealing with humanity, but I don't think what you believe is as important as that you believe. And when it comes to fixing your brain chemistry and putting your alcoholism into remission, I don't believe there to be any requirement for you to believe anything at all. Despite my own beliefs, I spend little time discussing religion when writing about addiction and recovery. I just see it as a tangential topic. For me, it is a very important topic in my life, but my spirituality was not the answer to my problems with alcoholism, so why would I offend people who don't share my beliefs? When asked why he doesn't comment on political issues, Michael Jordan famously said he stays out of politics because Republicans and Democrats both buy shoes. That's kind of how I feel. You and I don't need to be spiritually aligned for that which worked for me to work for you. So why take a chance on turning you off unnecessarily? Offending people is counterproductive to my goal of helping people find freedom from alcohol.

Alcoholism is not a spiritual deformity any more than it is a sign of weakness or a moral failing. Some of the most pious and upstanding of our citizens fall victim to alcohol addiction. When we ingest poison, bad things happen. Biologically and neurologically bad things, that is. Is that surprising? If you consider it logically without any preconceived notions about releasing our demons to a higher power, I don't think it should be. I just don't think we should confuse something that is of the utmost spiritual importance to us with a cure for our brain disease just because we hold our belief system in high regard.

If you had cancer, God would lovingly listen to all your prayers, but He'd probably be good with you seeing an oncologist, too.

Anonymity is Deadly

The anonymity offered to every person who walks into the rooms of Alcoholics Anonymous is the hook. It has long been considered the necessary incentive to encourage people to seek help, despite the shame they feel and the social stigma they perceive. I get it. Anonymity was not just an enticement; it was essential to creating a safe zone for people who worried about losing their jobs or reputations if word of their addiction got out.

As much as I understand the logical reason that anonymity has become the norm in early recovery from alcoholism, I also think anonymity's time has passed if we ever hope to defeat the stigma and bring the epidemic of alcohol addiction to an end. Even more important than the feeling of relative safety that anonymity brings, is the protection offered by a society that views alcoholism as a chronic disease with a medical treatment just like any other. The more open we are about our battles, the more we welcome others to open up as well.

My out loud recovery isn't just about the comfort I feel from the support of so many. It is much more about the invitation my story sends to many others to seek help and find the peace of sobriety. Alcoholism is such a selfish disease when we are actively drinking. What a relief it was for me to find the cure for my affliction, at least in part, in my openness about my struggles and the resulting benefit to others. In a way, we don't just defeat addiction with honesty. We also defeat selfishness with openness. Ask yourself this question: what would feel better, curing myself, or being part of the cure for millions?

I'm not suggesting for a minute that shouting out loud about our alcoholism and recovery is required in early sobriety. I was a year sober before I shared my story, and I'll tell you all about it in a later chapter. If this concept is paralyzing to consider, you are right where you belong. Before I was open, I protected my secret as though my life depended on it—because I thought it did. It didn't, but it sure seemed that way. The time will come for you to shout your own story, and you'll know it when it does. For now, all I'm asking is that we are open to the concept of openness, and that we recognize that anonymity feeds the stigma of shame and deceit. And since the stigma perpetuates the disease, the stigma is deadly.

Anonymity kills.

Nowhere in the rules and doctrine of Alcoholics Anonymous does it say that you can't share your own story of addiction and recovery. In AA, everyone who enters the rooms makes a mutual promise to protect the stories of each other. What is said in the rooms of AA stays in the rooms of AA, unless it is your own story, in which case, you are free to share it openly. In fact, most recovery warriors I know who believe in AA are open about their journeys and encourage others to do the same. I have resonated with so many of the people who are recovering in the rooms, and the support they have offered to me has been overwhelming.

Still, the promise of anonymity exists. Hard-core AA folks believe it is the cornerstone of the fellowship and reject my objection in its entirety. I'm not trying to be a contrarian who disagrees for disagreement's sake. I have no hatred for AA and believe that when it was written in the first half of the last century, *The Big Book* was the gospel of alcoholism, and revolutionized recovery at the time. But all good ideas run their course.

For every person saved by the protection of anonymity offered by AA, I believe many more wallow and suffer in ignorance. The anonymity of millions who recover in silence keeps an unknown number of people who are too ashamed, scared, weak or too proud to ask for help from asking. My story has led to salvation for others. I couldn't live with myself if I wasn't part of this broader solution.

Yes, there is a perceived value to anonymity. But at what cost to the society that turns so many of us into alcoholics in the first place?

The Answer Is in the Open Mind

Alcoholics Anonymous was not the solution for my disease. I do take issue with many of the foundational tenets of the organization. For instance, I do not find value in the amends process, as I explained in chapter six. However, even with all the areas in which AA is not a good fit for me, I celebrate the cumulative success of the program that has saved more lives than all other forms of addiction recovery combined.

AA has its place. For millions of people around the globe, it remains a valuable fellowship and process for recovery. There is room for AA in our modern world. But just as there is room for Alcoholics Anonymous, there is room for non-traditional, science-based options to attack this confounding affliction. AA is not the only way.

Some of the healthiest, most enlightened people I know have AA as a tool in their toolbox of sobriety. It is a part of their solution, but they also seek other modalities to help them find freedom. Many of them learn about brain chemistry, nutrition, exercise, meditation and so on to enhance their success in recovery. Those people make me happy just by their examples of well roundedness.

Some of the hardcore, staunch old guard of AA, however, do not share our open-minded approach. "We'll save you a seat at a meeting for when you relapse," I've been told more than a few times. "Shut up and get to a meeting," I've been ordered. "If you keep talking like this, you're going to kill someone. AA is the only proven method that works," I've been admonished.

Listen, I understand that my beliefs don't sit well with everyone. I know I rub people the wrong way. But here's the deal—what we're doing isn't working. Alcoholism remains an epidemic with more victims than those who suffer from cancer. We spend billions of dollars each year in the fight against cancer. It seems to me we should be open to some new ideas to address a disease with even more casualties.

Whatever you do to recover, I am proud of you. If this book is part of your solution, I am humbled and grateful. If AA provides you with everything you are looking for to find peace in sobriety, I remain eternally thankful for the fellowship. If you do nothing else while you try to unravel the mess alcohol has made of your life, I urge you to keep an open mind. Try all the options. Find your groove and go with it. Or encourage your loved one to experiment with the many recovery options available in this 21st century.

Whatever you do, don't become a narrow minded, know-it-all asshole. Someday, a new idea is going to eradicate the stigma. You don't want to be on the wrong side of innovation when that happens.

What Choice Did I have?

When it was time for me to get sober, I knew of only one
other recovery option besides AA, and it really wasn't an
option at all for me. Like so many, I had one of those jobs
that couldn't live without me. My wife and I owned our own
business, and we were active participants in the day-to-day
operations. If I had gone away to a 30-day inpatient treatment
facility, our business would have collapsed. The financial
disaster I had avoided through a decade of alcoholism would
have become unavoidable.

That's the thing about high-functioning alcoholism, our
condition is far more life-and-death than we are willing to
admit. Yet, one of the only two well-known treatment options
was easy to rule out for its invasiveness and collateral damage.

So, AA was not an option for me for its perceived
grotesqueness, and 30-day inpatient rehab wasn't an option
for its all-inclusiveness. I was hosed. Before I made my first
serious attempt to stop drinking, all the help that I was aware
of had been deemed unavailable for me. I was on my own.
At least, that's what I thought.

What might have been the case to a large degree in the
first two decades of the 21st century is no longer the case.
Lots of recovery warriors are doing great things out there, and
there are a wide variety of recovery options available to help
people no matter where they fall on the alcohol addiction
spectrum.

But you already know that, because you are reading this
book. Just because the help I found wasn't all organized in
one place, as it is now in this book, don't be mistaken. I did
not do this alone. I had help from some of the most
wonderful people I've ever met, and many who have no idea

I even exist. That mysterious sentence will be explained in future chapters. What is important is that you understand that you or your loved one can't do it alone. A formal program with meetings at designated places and times is not a requirement for recovery, but connection is absolutely, 100 percent necessary.

Sobriety is not the opposite of addiction. Do you know what is? Connection. Throughout the recovery community, there are lots of theories and pontifications. But there is one belief that is almost universally held: connection is the opposite of addiction.

And for you, maybe connection starts here, in the pages of this book. You are exploring new theories and trying different beliefs on for size. Engagement with these ideas can be the foundation of your connection to the recovery community, if you let it. There is much more to gain from sharing and interaction, but it can all start here.

If you are ready for more now, please consider our SHOUT Sobriety program for alcoholism recovery. We help people navigate the treacherous waters of early sobriety, and we offer tons of connection to others who know exactly how you feel.

SHOUTSobriety.com

If you are the loved one of someone suffering from alcoholism, we have a program for you, too. Echoes of Recovery is designed to help us share our stories and our pain and lean on and learn from one another. Just like AA is not a good fit for everyone, loved ones deserve more than one option to find support and healing in recovery.

EchoesOfRecovery.com

Both of these options are donation-based programs that are part of the nonprofit called Stigma (theStigma.org). There is no big up-front cost, we just request a small monthly recurring donation to keep our mission alive. If any of our participants stop finding value in what we offer, they can cancel their monthly subscription at any time.

The tools we employ in SHOUT Sobriety and Echoes of Recovery are the same methods of lasting sobriety explained in this book. Why not read the rest of the chapters, and decide if our programs might be a good fit for you?

Recovery from alcoholism was the second hardest thing I've ever done, and saving my marriage was even harder. I want the same freedom and enlightenment for you, and I don't want it to take you a decade to find. I hope what worked for me and my wife will work for you, whether you are a troubled drinker, or you love someone who is.

This is our story. This is our recovery. I hope it can help you find what you are looking for, too.

The feeling of relief washed over me like a little squirt of adrenaline making me tingle to the tips of my toes. I didn't drink. I made it through another night sober. The mornings of early sobriety always started with a slight lessening of the shame, a momentary sense of accomplishment before the weight of the stigma descended and I was reminded again that I was, in fact, still a hopeless alcoholic. That little injection of self-esteem was no match long-term against the feelings of shame and embarrassment that lingered, but it was enough to keep me going for a few hours at least.

I always felt better in the mornings in early sobriety. I was rested, of course. Often not fully rested, as the nightmares at the start of my recovery prevented me from getting anything close to a solid eight, or even seven hours of restorative sleep. But all that sleep was sober sleep. Which was better than the intoxicated unconsciousness for the first several hours of the night to which I had been accustomed.

The mornings were also better because drinking in the morning was not part of my routine. That's not to say that I never drank in the morning. On occasion, I did. Sometimes it was celebratory social morning drinking like on Christmas or tailgating before a college football game. More often than not, however, my morning drinking was extremely medicinal, intended to ease the pain of the debilitating depression I was trapped under. Either way, morning drinking had not invaded my habits and patterns for the start of the day, so my sobriety was both welcomed and expected before noon.

As the day wore on, I could feel the pressure, stress and disappointment build. Things sometimes didn't go as

planned at work. There were conversations that didn't feel
good or goals left unmet as time seemed to slip away. As the
hours ticked into the afternoon, achieving satisfaction grew
less likely, and contentment seemed to vanish. The end of
the workday approached, and the little victory of waking-up
sober lost all its shimmer and shine.

The witching hour. My witching hour. In the evenings
after a long day of work, the pull to drink alcohol was tugging
at me from every conceivable direction. It wasn't just a
psychological craving, although my brain was screaming for
the nightly ritual to which it had grown so accustomed. It was
logical to drink, too. Everyone drank after work. Everyone. I
was convinced of it. It was the American way, and it was my
right as a contributing member of society. Drinking was my
duty as an adult, as fundamental a right and expectation as
voting in elections and greeting my neighbors when I saw
them on the street. To not drink was an affront to my
responsibilities as an adult.

My witching hour was a real thing with cravings so
palpable I swear sometimes I could reach out and touch
temptation. The internal desire was matched by the societal
justification to create a force driving my actions like nothing
I'd ever experienced. It was like a tractor beam from a
science fiction movie, and resistance seemed futile.

For people who have never experienced addiction, the
witching hour is inconceivable. That an inanimate object can
have that much power over us is beyond their understanding.
Just don't drink. Sobriety is both as simple and as diabolically
complicated as those three words. Just don't drink. Fine. But
how? It might have been that simple, but it was also the
hardest thing I had ever done in my life.

Bibliotherapy

Surviving the witching hour was a daily battle for me. It was a fierce combat between my desired outcome (sobriety) and the instant gratification (drinking) that was incredibly familiar and accessible. There was pain. So much pain from shame and stigma, and I knew exactly how to make it vanish, at least temporarily. Relief was one drink away, but the battle lost would bring the shame raging back as a reminder of my ongoing failure. I had to end the cycle. I had to find relief free from destruction.

I don't remember how or why I started reading at my witching hour. I'm not sure how long it took me to realize that reading was a significant part of my solution to alcoholism. Maybe the passive nature of resonating with the words in a book is why it took me so long to accept the relief in those pages as important and lasting. Maybe the quiet solitude left the significance and healing hiding in plain sight.

Some people go to meetings during their witching hours. Others check into rehabs, thus relinquishing control of their routines and activities. Mostly though, people who need to banish alcohol from their lives give in and drink when temptation sets in, despite the known consequences. Until it worked for me, however, I'd never heard of anyone surviving their witching hour by curling up in a quiet room with a good book.

It is called bibliotherapy, and it's a real thing. Reading to keep the demons at bay is not my invention, but it was my salvation. It is seldom given the respect the technique deserves as a legitimate tool for recovery.

I read a lot in early recovery. I wanted to understand my disease. I wanted to learn about the ways I had poisoned my brain and body and understand my chances of making a full recovery with a dedication to permanent sobriety. Many of the books I read were clinical, and they gave me the technical information I needed to satisfy my craving for knowledge about my affliction. Those books were essential to my success, but they didn't scratch the itch when the witching hour was upon me like the memoirs of the alcoholics who had come before me and had the guts to write about it.

I read the stories of Caroline Knapp and Sarah Hepola and Augusten Burroughs and Pete Hamill and many more almost every night for months and months, until reading memoirs was the routine that replaced drinking. At the time, I was so private and secretive about my shameful dependence on alcohol, that I didn't dare discuss it with anyone but my wife, and frankly, she was sick of hearing about it. In those pages, I found understanding. In their words, I found stories to which I could relate and resonate. In their lives, I found compassion and understanding that had been previously unavailable in my life.

It is widely believed in the recovery community that connection is the opposite of addiction. Connection is why meetings work. Connection is why people get a sponsor and check in regularly.

But I have news for you: human connection is available through the gift of vulnerability. By laying their honest truths out in a raw and unfiltered way, the memoirists who told me their stories told my story, too. In doing so, they made me feel like I was not alone. They made me realize I was not a weak and depraved subhuman creature. They gave me hope, and they made sobriety and healing real. Their choice and success in sobriety contradicted everything society had ever taught me about the relationship between alcohol and adulthood. They made my recovery a real and respectable possibility. And that is connection.

Have you ever loved someone who doesn't know you exist? I have. All the storytellers who had the fearlessness to speak their truths showed me a love I'd never felt before, and the connection I feel to them is as real and tangible as any other connection I've been blessed to experience. I owe them my life, and they don't even know me.

Am I being too dramatic? Is my over-the-top description of the emotions I feel for the authors who wrote about their addiction and recovery for my benefit too much? Maybe. But here's the point. When I tell people how important reading was to my recovery, the typical response is, "Yeah, great, reading. What else did you do to get sober?" Bibliotherapy is consistently blown-off as a minor player in the battle against an epidemic disease. "You read to get sober? I'll save a seat for you at AA for when you relapse." I've heard that more than a few times.

I get it. Bibliotherapy is nontraditional, and it feels like it is not substantial enough to be taken seriously. It is like tomato soup for dinner. It tastes great, but where are the meat and potatoes? Reading feels like a side dish, not the main entrée.

Reading memoirs saved my life. It is that simple. If my approach to recovery is to work for you or the alcoholic you love, reading is to be taken seriously and prioritized over everything when the witching hour strikes. Reading is not an accent to be indulged when life affords some extra time. It is vital to successful recovery. In early sobriety, reading assumed the role alcohol once had in my life. Reading nightly came first.

Recommended Reading

There are hundreds of excellent memoirs available to provide you the connection necessary for your success in recovery. Likewise, there are lots of clinical books that offer readers the biological and neurological details they desire to understand the disease of alcoholism. I have read a lot of them, and I offer here a variety of suggestions. I recommend that you add these to your personal library. If you need to quit drinking, or if you want to better understand the inner turmoil that your beloved drinker is experiencing, these books will help.

Some touched me more deeply than others. Please check out the descriptions I provide as a starting point for which books to read first. There is a good deal of variety in my recommended reading list. I'm confident you'll find multiple stories to help you, or the drinker you love, through the witching hour.

Drinking: A Love Story, by Caroline Knapp
This is the all-time best alcoholism memoir written by the godmother of the genre. I've read it easily 10 times, and I get chills just thinking about how it changed my life. Caroline is a magnificent writer, the writer I hope to someday grow to be. Her descriptors, scene setting, humility, vulnerability and complete honesty draws me in like I am reading my own story. Even the section about her eating disorder is transfixing, and I didn't even know how to spell anorexia before I read this book. While it is brutal in its honest reality, it is also tender and chick-y. If you or the drinker you love is overly masculine, it might not hit the spot (although it's so good, that I bet secretly, it will).

Blackout: Remembering the Things I Drank to Forget, by
Sarah Hepola
If Caroline Knapp is the godmother, Sarah Hepola is her
godchild. Her writing is edgy and graphic and descriptive and
painful, and her story resonates with my soul. The first half of
the book is about her drinking, while the second half is about
the challenges of her recovery. Right in the middle, there is a
tiny section of transition where she describes crawling into
her closet with a blanket in the middle of the night—night
after night—and curling into a ball with her hopeless, dismal
discomfort. Her bottom was my bottom, and I cry just
thinking about how those few desperate pages jammed
between misery and hope saved my life. Sarah is quite a bit
more brash than Caroline. The prelude to the book opens
with Sarah coming out of a blackout, naked on top of a
strange man in his unfamiliar hotel room. This prelude
inspired me to be so brutally honest and vulnerable in the
prelude to my book that you are reading now (thank you).

Dry: A Memoir, by Augusten Burroughs
Like Caroline and Sarah, Augusten is just a master of his
craft. This book is a detailed and entrancing tale about an
advertising executive and his fall from grace at the hands of
the drink. The greedy and obsessive way he drank in the
depths of his addiction is sad and riveting. If you or the
drinker you love might enjoy getting wrapped up in
exceptional prose with a bit of humility and humor, Augusten
delivers.

A Drinking Life: A Memoir, by Pete Hamill
Toward the end of his career as an accomplished and
acclaimed writer, Pete wrote this memoir about how

drinking—heavy drinking—was intertwined throughout his life
from childhood until he finally quit cold turkey. It is
interesting and well written by an excellent storyteller. My
only beef with this book is that it ends abruptly when he quits
drinking. I wanted, no, I needed to hear about a recovery
warrior overcoming shame and other challenges in an
alcohol-soaked world, and this book is unfulfilling in that
regard. But if you, or the person you love who drinks too
much, might benefit from the story of a life of adventure
floating on a river of ever-present booze that left the writer
with enough damage done to convince him to leave the drink
behind, this book might be helpful at the witching hour.

Unwasted: My Lush Sobriety, by Sacha Z. Scoblic
Sacha tells the story of going to a bar one evening for a drink
(as in one drink) and emerging at 7:30 a.m. with the sun
burning her eyes and barely enough time to stumble into
work. On this list, Sacha is the fifth consecutive purely
exquisite writer. She was a wild adventurer in college who
never matured as long as booze was there to stunt her growth,
and that is a quality that is most definitely relatable for me.
Like Caroline's and Sarah's work, I have read this one many
times because Sacha is the female version of me, and I love
her for telling our story.

We are the Luckiest, by Laura McKowen
This is the only book on my list that was published after I was
years into my recovery. Although it was not directly
responsible for my permanent sobriety, Laura is a brilliant
writer with an unmatched ability to connect with her readers.
While this is the story of her drinking life, it is not straight
memoir. She tells stories of her personal experience, and

then offers readers advice. This style is prescriptive with a whole lot of real-life experience to back up her assertions. Laura is a powerful leader in the sobriety revolution, and her book will not disappoint.

The Sobering Truth: What You Don't Know Can Kill You, by Dr. Jeff Herten

The incident Jeff considers his rock bottom took place when he disciplined a rambunctious child at an adult party by grabbing the kid's shoulder to get his attention. He wasn't drunk, but beer was definitely in control of the situation, and it was creating chaos in Jeff's life. When Jeff was confronted by the child's mom in the morning, he was devastated and decided enough was enough. This book is a well-written blend of clinical information of how alcohol poisons the various systems of our body, and Jeff's personal experiences both as a drinker and a medical doctor who treated alcohol-abusing patients. It provides valuable, factual information with a personal, vulnerable twist. This is an excellent, well rounded book for anyone who benefits from facts to provide context to our emotions.

Understanding the High-Functioning Alcoholic, by Sarah Allen Benton

Much like Dr. Jeff's book, Sarah's contribution to the genre twists her personal struggles with alcohol addiction into a clinical description of the stages of high-functioning alcoholism. While Sarah bravely shares many personal details for the benefit of her readers on a topic to which she has dedicated her life, much of the explanation is medical and somewhat dry. If you value clinical knowledge over the touchy-feely stuff, this is an outstanding read on the complicated and misunderstood subject of addiction.

Living Sober Sucks (but living drunk sucks more), by Mark A. Tuschel

This was the first book I ever read about alcoholism, and it deserves a place on this list even though I struggle to resonate with Mark's tale of outwardly obnoxious drug and alcohol abuse. This is a manly man's tale of getting wasted while mowing the lawn and doing projects around the house, wrecking his boat into his dock and having an affair in Las Vegas. Mark turned from proud and brazen drunk to weeping, suicidal shell-of-his-former-self in an early recovery that included a divorce from his wife who considered him weak for giving up the booze. If you or the drinker you love makes no attempt to hide the party 24/7 lifestyle, this is the book for you. Mark's open and unapologetic tale will hit home for drinkers who wear public drunkenness as a badge of honor.

Drunk on Sports, by Tim Cowlishaw

Tim is a sportswriter in Texas who argues his opinion regularly on ESPN. In his pseudo-celebrity tell-all, Tim explains how drinking opened doors in his journalistic career. And how it made conversations, and thus sports scoops, available as he bellied-up to the bar with coaches, players and team owners. This was the second book I read about alcoholism, and it was a bit confusing. While Tim admits that sobriety saved his uncontrollable life, he also tells us he could not have reached the pinnacle of his writing career without his willingness to drink. Although this book was less helpful to me than other books on this list when my goal was survival of early sobriety, I included it for one reason. If you or the drinker you love is a sports nut, Tim Cowlishaw will likely be a familiar name and voice. When we are trying to help troubled drinkers, we have to meet them where they live. If you live on ESPN, buy this book.

Reading is Serious Business

We think of reading as a leisurely pastime or an academic endeavor. But there is a third purpose for reading. It can be wildly therapeutic and help us unravel the mystery of the neurological hijacking that threatens to destroy every aspect of our lives. Reading can be effective in ways that expand far beyond entertainment and education. Reading saved my life.

I read all the books reviewed above in the eBook format on my smartphone's Kindle app. I recommend this format for books to get you through the witching hour for three reasons.

First, and most unfortunately, reading about alcoholism is still a stigmatized and shameful thing in early recovery. I could read on airplanes, while waiting for my kids' basketball practice to end, or in any other public venue without feeling the need to obscure the outside cover of the book I was reading. Reading using my Kindle app assured my privacy.

Second, my books were always in my pocket and available in the case of a temptation emergency. For bibliotherapy to be effective, the reading material must be consistently and easily accessible. Like a rescue inhaler for my neurological version of asthma, even a quick page or two kept me from making bad decisions when faced with unexpected temptation on many occasions. It is just impossible for a hard copy book to be as accessible.

Third, I have re-read most of the books on my suggested reading list. Several of them, I have read over a dozen times. You can certainly re-read a hard copy book, too, but boy is it easy to go back to a previously devoured eBook masterpiece when you don't have to get out of bed to do so, or when you finish a book while traveling where it would be inconvenient to buy another book to read. Because books are a vital component of recovery from alcoholism, anything that can be done to make reading easy is a major asset.

The downside to reading eBooks on our smartphones is that they cannot be shared with others when we've finished them. Oh wait, I'm a published book author. That isn't a downside, that means more book sales when someone buys a copy of my book (because they loved it) for a friend (who they also love). I am looking at this all wrong. And if you think this makes me greedy, maybe reconsider how you are looking at the situation, too. Think of all the money you or your loved one might be spending on booze if not reading when temptation strikes instead. You buying books is a financial win/win for both of us.

Books used for bibliotherapy are much more than a $15 paperweight. They are comforting. They are connection. Books can save lives. I hope you understand the impact. I hope that's why you're reading my book. I hope it is the salvation for you, or the over-drinker in your life, that reading through the witching hour was for me.

I've heard stories of people who found themselves sitting in their cars in liquor store parking lots, drinking their new purchases, with no idea how they got there or why. These were people who were committed to long-term sobriety and seemed moved by a mystical force to drink against their will. That never happened to me. I had plenty of relapses before I made it over the elusive and invisible hump to permanent sobriety, but mine were all quite intentional. I never found myself drinking and wondered why. I had what I thought was a justifiable reason each time I tried to control my drinking. Even though I thought I knew why, I now know that I had no idea what was going on in my brain, what made me restart my relationship with booze over a half-dozen times during my decade of active alcoholism.

About a year before I quit drinking for good, I made it to nine months of sobriety. I still felt awful. I was depressed all the time. I didn't have the crash and burn type of depression that always accompanied a Monday morning after a weekend of hitting it hard, but I was just never happy and never content. Success at work, things that were supposed to be fun with the family, even watching or playing sports, none of it brought me any pleasure. My life felt a lot like living in a cold gray sock. Even at nine months, long-term sobriety had revealed surprisingly few benefits, and I made the conscious and deliberate decision to try to control my drinking once again. If I was going to be miserable either way, my logic dictated that I might as well try to get a little pleasure out of alcohol.

In both real and common examples of relapse, we alcoholics don't understand what's going on in our gray matter to drive the decision to drink. We think ourselves weak and deviant. We don't understand that we have a neurological disorder caused by our consistent consumption of poison. We are not, in fact, cretins who lack willpower. Our brains are adapting to one of the world's most highly addictive substances in just the way they were designed. Addiction is a brain disease, and both relapse examples are classic cases of how alcoholism works.

Reading was such a vital part of my early recovery, and memoirs—the stories of the alcoholics who came before me and found healing freedom—were my main source of reading material. But in addition to connecting to those stories, I also found great comfort in learning about the changes to my brain chemistry that my infatuation with alcohol created over time. Learning about brain chemistry helped me feel less like a weak pariah and more like the victim of a chronic disease like cancer, diabetes or heart disease. Did my decisions to drink bring on my affliction? Absolutely. Does that mean the faulty rewiring of my brain wasn't a real, legitimate condition? Absolutely not. And diseases have treatments. Treating my disease gave me hope that was not available when I thought I was dealing with a moral failing or character defect.

Neurotransmitter Hijacking

There are two distinct parts of the brain chemistry equation that are the most applicable to me when trying to understand the neurological condition of addiction. The first is the hijacking of our pleasure chemicals that takes place when we drink heavily, or at least consistently, for an extended period of time. The chemicals that send signals around our craniums, and result in our feelings and behaviors, are called neurotransmitters. And the four neurotransmitters that are associated with pleasure are dopamine, serotonin, gaba and endorphins.

You've probably heard of dopamine. It is the most often highlighted of the pleasure neurotransmitters, and it is a topic in a wide range of subjects expanding far beyond addiction into any discussion of mental health. We often talk about, "dopamine hits," coming from pleasurable activities. I have a mental image of my brain in a public bathroom with lines of powdered dopamine segmented carefully on a vanity mirror with a razor blade snorting the neurotransmitter through a rolled-up hundred-dollar bill. That's not at all how it works, but the mental picture effectively conveys the accurate imagery.

Dopamine is the rock star of the neurotransmitters because it has such versatility and is affected by all addictive behaviors. One of the reasons alcohol is so highly addictive is that it hijacks not just one or two of the pleasure neurotransmitters, but it warps the release of dopamine, serotonin, gaba and endorphins. Alcohol's overwhelming success as an addictive substance can be attributed to its wide-ranging cranial impact.

I have learned the distinction between the four pleasure neurotransmitters on a dozen or more occasions, and frankly, I keep forgetting the details. To me, this is a sign that for an alcoholic in recovery, or anyone who loves a person battling alcohol addiction, the detailed differences between how dopamine and serotonin work, for example, is not important.

If you are a neuroscientist, you already know the difference. If you are not, you don't really need to, so I'm not going to waste your time.

What I am going to share is really important. Before your eyes gloss over as I start explaining brain chemistry, please understand that I'm only going to cover the most relevant topics that will have a transformative effect on your ability to understand permanent sobriety and enlightenment. Without this information, I would not have been able to return my brain to near-normal function and heal. I'm not a scientist, and I have only the level of interest in this topic that anyone has about their specific affliction when they receive a particular diagnosis. I won't try to lose you in the weeds. I'll only share that which I found vital to my ability to recover.

Here's how the brain chemistry hijacking works. When we drink, we feel good. That is our brain releasing the pleasure neurotransmitters. At the beginning, our brains release these chemicals in response to a variety of joyful inputs. When we kiss someone we love, watch a beautiful sunset, dip our toes in the ocean, see our kids perform well at a band concert, receive an unexpected compliment or finish that first IPA, we get a little jolt of happy courtesy of our pleasure neurotransmitters.

But as we continue to drink alcohol regularly and in significant quantities, a problem develops. Our brains are constantly trying to reach a state of equilibrium called homeostasis. This equilibrium is vital to our survival. Too much or too little of any of the components that keep us alive will throw us out of balance, and our brains are hardwired to take sometimes drastic measures to return us to homeostasis. Picture an old-school playground teeter-totter. Our brains are trying to keep that board perfectly parallel with the ground at all times, while we flail around going up and down and creating massive stressors for our own melons.

As our brains begin to make a solid association between alcohol and pleasure, we begin to reserve that neurotransmitter release for only when alcohol enters our system. When we drink regularly, and also see sunsets and feel pride for our kids and eat great meals and have sex, it is simply more pleasure than our brains will allow, and we begin to down-regulate the release of dopamine and the others neurotransmitters.

We teach our brains to withhold pleasure neurotransmitters for alcohol consumption only. No drink, no pleasure. And that, in easily understandable terms, is addiction.

It took me years, even decades, to warp the relationship between alcohol and pleasure into a straight line, a one-to-one connection. When I was fully experiencing active addiction to alcohol, booze was one of the only things that brought me relief or pleasure (sexual orgasm was the only other consistent and tangible activity that brought me a brief respite of joyful neurotransmitter release).

The achievements of my kids, a smile or hug from my wife, a win for my favorite sports team, a financial success— none of it made me feel good the way it should have. My ability to feel pleasure was completely hijacked by booze. Alcohol entering my system had become required for the release of dopamine, serotonin, gaba and endorphins. I was a prisoner of my own dedication to drinking.

Probably the most common collateral damages associated with alcoholism are depression and anxiety. Because they creep up slowly in coordination with our brain chemistry hijacking, we often don't even realize the worsening depression and anxiety we are experiencing are a result of our drinking. This is both logical, and also a little-known fact of drinking. Depression and anxiety are the natural antithesis of pleasure. No release of those four neurotransmitters means sadness and an elevated sense of doom. That's certainly what happened in my case. In the last few years of my active alcoholism, I suffered a debilitating depression that was completely out of control. Likewise, I stressed and worried about every little thing. My mind was almost never at peace. I developed obsessive-compulsive disorder that made locking down our little single-story bungalow a painful chore that took half an hour or more. I was a mess, and I had no idea alcohol was causing my growing levels of mental distress.

Quite to the contrary. I knew that when I felt depressed or under a burden of anxiety, drinking brought temporary relief. That was the release of pleasure chemicals reserved only for alcohol. When panic ensued, I drank alcohol, and it went temporarily away. That association was direct and easy to make. That the depression and anxiety came raging back with ever-increasing frequency and severity was an association with alcohol that eluded me. I had no idea my drinking was harming my mental health. I only knew booze was the elixir that brought relief. This is where the term for alcohol as a, "self-medication," comes from.

This is also why alcoholism is a progressive disease. As the negative consequences of our drinking increase, so does the perceived benefit we find in self-medicating. This often results in breaking our own rules associated with our drinking. Robin Williams famously said, "As an alcoholic, you will violate your standards quicker than you will lower them." That certainly was the case for me.

I would never have considered drinking in the morning on a workday...until I did. Some Monday mornings were so brutal, so filled with crushing depression and anxiety, that I was forced to turn to the only sure form of relief I knew. I drank vodka and nursed my brain back to sanity and human function. It is despicable and disgusting to look back at how far I truly fell, while maintaining the outward appearance of holding it all together. But that's what happened to me as my disease progressed, and it's what happened to Robin Williams and millions of other high-functioning alcoholics. We chase with alcohol the relief for that pain our drinking is causing. The cycle is as insidious as it is completely misunderstood.

The Subconscious Mind

The second part of the brain chemistry hijacking happens very much on a subconscious level. When I write or talk about this part, I often feel people's eyes rolling as though I'm describing some ghostly spiritual possession. We give so little thought or credit to the power of our subconscious minds, that it is considered a weakness not to be able to control every aspect of our brain function.

Maybe think about it this way, though. Do you consciously control your breathing or your eye blinking? How about your heart rate? Do you make the conscious decision to sweat when you are hot or catch yourself when you lose balance? Do you give a lot of thought to food digestion or releasing mucus to fight unwelcome nasal intruders? No? That's because your subconscious mind takes care of all of that stuff, leaving the part of your brain you control for thinking and making bad decisions (and lots of good ones, too, like reading this book). Our subconscious minds are powerful—in a way that really can't be overstated. Alcoholism is stigmatized as an affliction of weakness. Nothing could be further from the truth. When we effectively and efficiently train our brains to associate alcohol with pleasure, the connection is strong, and our powerful subconscious shows great strength to enforce that connection.

Alcoholism isn't a sign of weakness. Rather, it is a show of strength: our subconscious mind flexing our neuro-muscles and executing the tactics we taught it.

Our human brains consider pleasure to be required for survival. It is right up there with food, shelter and love as one of the necessities, and our subconscious mind will drive us to find the pleasure we need.

When we make the association between pleasure and alcohol through years of drinking and neurotransmitter down-regulation as just described, we identify alcohol as an essential component for survival. If pleasure is required, and alcohol is the only thing in our lives that provides pleasure, alcohol is required. I knew that logic class I loved in college would come in handy someday.

I opened this chapter with an often-repeated story about alcoholics in early recovery who find themselves drinking when they had no intention of doing so, and sometimes don't even remember procuring the booze. They don't remember and have no control because their powerful subconscious minds are trying to survive by ingesting alcohol.

To someone who has never experienced addiction, this might sound like a cop out. "My inner demons made me drink. I didn't want to do it. It wasn't really me." This is also why *The Big Book of Alcoholics Anonymous*, written over 80 years ago, considers alcoholism to be a spiritual deficiency. We didn't understand neuroscience back then. Without a scientific understanding of the subconscious mind, of course we have to call addiction a moral failing. It is the only other explanation that holds water. But it is wrong. Alcoholism isn't a weakness in spirituality. It is a learned behavior—an ingrained neurological association.

It is well known throughout the addiction recovery community that we should try never to get too hungry, too thirsty, too tired, or too stressed, because any one of those physiological deficiencies can lead to relapse. When alcoholism is described as a spiritual problem, the reason for relapse in one of those vulnerable conditions is hard to explain. But when we understand that our subconscious mind associates alcohol with survival, it is obvious why hunger or exhaustion would cause us intense cravings to drink. When we need something, our brain goes into survival mode and procures for us anything related to survival. If you are dehydrated and stressed out, your brain is going to do anything possible to make you drink. It's not spiritual. It is neurobiological.

Our subconscious mind is also where our routines and patterns live. For many years, I drank alcohol after work on the weekdays, and any time after noon on the weekends. So my witching hours, the times when I most craved alcohol when I was in early sobriety, were weekday evenings and weekend afternoons. These patterns, once grooved into our subconscious, are extremely difficult to change.

I didn't know it at the time, but my dedication to bibliotherapy helped me defeat the witching hour cravings because I was so consistent with my new reading habit. Had I done a variety of different white-knuckled activities every evening, I would have been fighting the routine, but I would not have been introducing a new pattern as a replacement. By consistently reading through the witching hour, I was establishing a new routine at the same time as I was trying to abolish an old one that was causing me harm.

As previously explained, our subconscious minds are extremely strong. Trying to overcome them without giving them some replacement tactics to latch onto is an exercise in futility. Reading in the evenings became a replacement for drinking, and a regular, nightly tradition that I even started to crave as the afternoon rolled on.

A Poison in Any Quantity

Think for a minute about what is actually happening in our brains when we drink alcohol. Besides the neurotransmitter hijacking, and reprogramming of our subconscious minds, we are inhibiting proper brain function. A stumbling drunk has lost motor skills, cognitive function, social restraint and emotional control. We basically strangle our brains when we drink.

When we drink a lot, this asphyxiation of brain cells is obvious. But even at lower consumption levels, like when we feel a nice buzz, that sensation is the result of taking our most precious organ when operating properly and poisoning it so it slows and glitches. When I put it that way, catching a buzz doesn't seem quite so desirable, does it?

I cite often that there are over 15 million alcoholics in America. That means there are over 100 million American drinkers who believe they drink in moderation, and that alcohol is serving them. There's one major problem with that assumption.

In permanent sobriety, some tremendous things started to happen for me as my brain chemistry returned to near normal. My depression didn't just decrease, it disappeared altogether. I still have times of natural sadness, but I don't experience anything close to the clinical depression I suffered as an active alcoholic. Likewise, my anxiety disappeared, and now it only takes me a few minutes to lock down our little house every night.

Do you know how many people take antidepressants, anti-anxiety meds and sleeping pills in the United States alone? Many, many millions. For some, these medications are lifesaving and necessary. But for many of them, the solution to their problem is to stop drinking their daily cocktail of despair. Alcohol is a depressant. Before you accept a prescription for an antidepressant, shouldn't you remove the depressant from your life and see if that cures what ails you? Alcohol creates anxiety, and disrupts sleep patterns, too. Doesn't it make more sense to experiment with sobriety than to medicate the problems drinking might be causing?

I know people who are control freaks, have short tempers and seem unable to relax. The people I'm thinking about, who struggle with these unfortunate personality traits, are also drinkers. What if? What would happen if they stopped poisoning their brains on a regular basis? My depression and anxiety were eliminated in sobriety. I wonder how many "moderate" drinkers walk around everyday trying to hold their lives together while their controlled drinking hinders their mental health.

Alcohol is a poison in any quantity. Period. There is no safe quantity of alcohol. This is a fact lost on the vast majority of our population who will drink themselves into a slightly unfulfilled state of existence all the way to their graves. They are proud of their ability to control their drinking. They conform to societal norms, and love catching that brain-function-inhibiting buzz. And they have no idea how much better their lives could be.

One of the most critical components of my permanent sobriety is my understanding that alcohol is a poison without redeeming qualities. I no longer wish I was able to moderate my drinking. I am not jealous of the people who can drink one or two and then quit. In fact, I feel sorry for those people. They don't know how much better their human experience could be.

Alcohol is a poison. Drinking a little poison is in no way better than drinking no poison at all. I'm sure there is a quantity of Drano you could drink, too, but I have no desire to find out how much that is!

Patience

I have good news and good news about repairing our brain chemistry. What would you like first? The good news, you say. Great! The good news is that our subconscious minds, that we so painstakingly trained over years and gallons of booze, can be retrained. Breaking the ingrained associations and creating new patterns is not easy, and it is not done overnight, but it can be done.

We can restore our neurotransmitters to near-normal function as well. That's the other good news. Over time, our brains will go back to releasing pleasure neurotransmitters for the other little joys in life unrelated to alcohol consumption.

I use the term, "near-normal function," because the patterns we groove in active addiction to alcohol are never really reversed. Just as cancer can go into remission, our alcoholic brain chemistry can be put into dormancy. As long as we don't drink, it will stay that way, and our dopamine, serotonin, gaba and endorphins will fire on all cylinders for the rest of our sober lives.

But if we ever drink again, our cunning and sophisticated brains will search our memory banks for what to do with the alcohol we are ingesting. The neurotransmitter dysfunction is dusted off and put back into service, while our subconscious mind re-associates alcohol with survival. And after years or decades of sobriety, the return of the alcoholic brain only takes a few days, or even a few hours. There are countless cases of people who thought they "fixed" themselves or "reset" their brains in sobriety. Such belief is a painful myth with devastating consequences. It just cannot happen.

I've repeatedly watched a Robin Williams interview (can you tell I'm infatuated with his story) conducted by David Letterman where Robin explains that after 20 years of sobriety, he decided to try to drink again. After just a couple of days back to drinking, his consumption and behavior was in a worse state of chaos than in his last days of drinking two decades prior.

Alcoholism is a progressive disease. It can only get worse with no hope of ever being cured. That is a definitive statement.

If you stop drinking, you can find the healing and enlightenment we all deserve. That's certainly what happened to me over an extended period of time. The idea of changing back into a moderate drinker is a complete farce that has been proven impossible countless times with such sad consequences.

The concepts of addiction transference and harm reduction have been practiced in traditional addiction recovery for many, many years. The basic idea is that if an alcoholic transfers their addiction to a less harmful behavior, that is a good thing. Now that we understand brain chemistry, addiction transference isn't as beneficial as it is cracked up to be.

With the increasing number of states legalizing marijuana, weed is often substituted by people who want to quit drinking alcohol. Booze, generally speaking, tends to create anger in people where marijuana creates sluggish lethargy. Since lazy people are, on the surface, less harmful to the people they love than mean people, many drinkers are happy to transfer their alcoholism into an addiction to marijuana.

Here's one of the many problems with this strategy that I want to highlight in this chapter on brain chemistry: Weed has the same hijacking effect on dopamine that alcohol has. Smoking marijuana instead of drinking alcohol does not allow our brains to heal and return to near-normal function. It also does not allow our subconscious mind to develop new patterns. When we use weed in place of drinking, we perpetuate the same damage, and never make healthy progress. Changing from an asshole to a slug is hardly a desirable transformation, especially since it doesn't do a thing to address our underlying alcoholism.

Trading one bad thing for another is not a goal with estimable results. Permanent sobriety, and the enlightenment of recovery, are the only conclusions that are worth the effort of defeating alcoholism. And nothing is more important to our goal of finding that peace and freedom than patience. I'm not talking about waiting to see what's under the Christmas tree on the morning of December 25th. I'm talking about real, sustained and unimaginably challenging patience—the kind of patience that is not accessible to most of us when we are active drinkers.

I started this chapter with a story about a relapse I experienced after nine months of sobriety. I also made it to six months on two different occasions before I returned to my alcoholic routine. Why didn't I feel better after so much continuous sobriety? I thought that if I made it that long, and the depression and anxiety were still unbearable, I was not going to heal, so drinking to medicate seemed like a reasonable decision.

The simple fact is that for most alcoholics, six months is not long enough. Neither is nine months. Most alcoholics in recovery report the start of significant brain function changes after a year or more of continuous sobriety. My experience is certainly in line with that generalization. It takes a long time to begin to recover from alcoholism.

I know how disappointing this news might be. I certainly wasn't interested in a year-long process to even start to find improvement when it was time for me to get sober. But looking back, it really wasn't too steep a price to pay. I drank, and drank hard, for 25 years. Who the hell did I think I was to expect that neuro-damage to be repaired in a matter of months? If I spent 25 years digging a hole, why on earth would I expect to climb out in nine short months. The damage of alcoholism is real and relentless, and defeating the monster, even the monster in our heads—no, especially the neurological monster in our heads—takes time. Serious, prolonged amounts of patiently recovering time.

It can be done. I did it, and so have millions of others. The biggest mistake you can make is underestimating the task of recovery, both from the standpoint of effort, and patience required. If you are an alcoholic in early recovery, please recognize that you have a lot of miles on a long road ahead. If you love an alcoholic, please work to find the patience to give the recovery process room to breathe.

Here's some more good news: repairing brain chemistry is arduous work, and it takes a long time, but it is definitely worth the effort to find pleasure in pleasurable things, once again.

No poison required.

chapter 10 | what you eat can cure you

In the late 90s, I lost 40 pounds on a low-fat diet. There are a lot of decisions and factors that resulted in my addiction to alcohol, but this period of weight loss had an incredibly significant impact on my crossing into alcoholism. Low-fat diets were all the rage for basically the last two decades of the 20th century. But low fat also meant high carb, at least for me. My go-to snack was fat-free pretzels dipped in fat-free cream cheese, and I basically allowed myself unlimited quantities. The pretzels were made from refined white flour: simple carbs without fiber or any nutritional benefit. The fat in the cream cheese was replaced by sugars, chemicals and fillers.

The other thing I allowed myself, in basically unlimited quantities during this period of weight loss, was vodka. I was working out twice a day and I had severely limited my diet, so I felt I deserved the reward. Without really doing any research, I had this notion that vodka was less fattening than beer. The clear liquid just looked cleaner and harmless to my mind that was fixated on dropping my love handles. They don't call the fat-mass I had hanging over my belt a "vodka belly," so the beer mostly had to go. Mostly.

What I didn't know until I was almost two years into my alcoholism recovery was that my diet from the late 90s, headlined by fat-free pretzels, fat-free cream cheese and vodka, had carved addiction pathways into my brain. Sugars, refined carbs (which our bodies process in such a way as to make them the nutritional equivalent of sugars) and alcohol all trigger our neurotransmitters in basically the same way. When those three inputs made up the majority of my diet,

they cut deep grooves into my neurological system. The
sugar, simple carbs and alcohol taught my brain to release
pleasure neurotransmitters. Especially because the weight was
falling off me, I did feel good about myself when I restricted
my diet in that way. My snack, and the vodka I often washed
it down with, hijacked my reward system. Sugar, refined flour
and vodka propelled me toward my alcoholic inevitability.
Going back even further, my nutritional mistakes made
alcohol addiction my destiny long before the late 90s. As a
kid, when I came home from school, I almost always wolfed
down like half a bag of Doritos before doing my homework. I
am a product of the first, true, processed food generation.
Our parents thought the convenience offered by innovation
was miraculous, and no one considered the nutritional
consequences at the time. But of course, there was collateral
damage. Doritos were simple carbs with sugar added to make
them addictive. I started carving the neural pathways that
alcohol would eventually flow down long before I had my
first drink. If I wasn't born an alcoholic, I sure was an
overachiever working on my addiction way back in
elementary school.

Nutrition matters. A lot. People often debate whether
addiction is genetic or environmental. Alcoholism is often
characterized as a spiritual deficiency. The truth is, we are
what we eat, and alcoholism is a self-inflicted condition that
can start well in advance of taking a pledge of allegiance to
the bottle.

Alcohol's Ugly Stepsister

Nutrition matters even more in alcoholism recovery. The
neural pathways that we groove in recovery can't necessarily

undo damage done in active alcoholism. But we can make new cranial connections that help us regenerate depleted dopamine, serotonin, gaba and endorphins.

Alcoholics in early recovery almost universally report increased cravings for sugar. Given what you have just learned, it makes sense, doesn't it? When we refuse to give our bodies the alcohol we desire, our brains start to scream for the next best thing—a substance that fits that same groove.

When we consume a lot of sugar early in our sobriety, it does two things: sugar calms the cravings for now, and it ensures that the cravings for alcohol or sugar will come roaring back later.

A good friend of mine, and licensed addiction therapist, was a proponent of the 12-Steps and traditional forms of addiction treatment. As part of his practice, he would recommend to clients struggling with severe alcohol cravings that they go to Dairy Queen and treat themselves to their favorite flavor of Blizzard whenever the cravings became intense. He was proud of the effectiveness of the advice, as his clients often reported that the Blizzard kept them away from the bottle for that moment. When he learned what I learned about sugar and our neurotransmitters, he was astonished and immediately stopped recommending the Blizzard treatment.

Just because sugar offers immediate comfort, we ignore the long-term effects at our own peril. I'm not even talking about the nutritional risk of increasing our chances of getting diabetes, cancer or heart disease. I'm talking about the major barrier sugar presents to balancing our brain chemistries and returning to near-normal function. It is much the same as when people switch from drinking alcohol to smoking marijuana. Nothing gets fixed. The neural dysfunction just gets fed a different poison. Our disease continues to thrive.

Therefore, relapses are so common with traditional methods of addiction recovery. Until recently, we didn't understand the relationship between alcohol and sugar. Brain chemistry is the final frontier of human biology. Innovation and discovery are to be fully expected. What is completely unexplainable is why traditional forms of addiction recovery don't incorporate what we are learning now into their methods. This is not minor stuff. This is a total game changer. More importantly, if widely adopted, avoiding added sugar and simple carbs in early recovery will be a lifesaver!

Blood Sugar and Relapse

Sugar and simple carbs play another dastardly role in slowing or preventing alcoholism recovery. As we've discussed, our brains and bodies are in a constant quest for homeostasis. That applies to our desired blood-sugar levels as well. When we eat a balanced and nutritious meal with lots of vegetables, proteins and fats, our blood sugar rises, but stays within our body's normal range. Our pancreas releases insulin to bring our blood sugar safely and calmly back down to the desired level. The process takes place in just the way the human brain and body are designed to manage food intake.

When we eat calories that are high in added sugars or refined carbs, however, our blood sugar spikes, throwing our bodies out of equilibrium. Our brains react to the emergency by releasing massive amounts of insulin to bring our spiked blood sugar down rapidly. The insulin released is an overcorrection, and our blood sugar overshoots the normal, desired mark, and falls dangerously low.

When our blood sugar drops below safe levels, our brains go into survival mode, and move decision-making from our prefrontal cortex, the part of our brains where normal, logical, rational conclusions are reached, to our animal brain called the amygdala. The amygdala is the part of our brains where impulsive survival decisions are made. The amygdala is responsible for fight or flight reactions. When our blood sugar is dangerously low, our animal brains send us on a search for inputs that we have linked to survival.

As we learned in the chapter on brain chemistry, because pleasure neurotransmitters, for us alcoholics, are only released when we consume alcohol, and pleasure is considered necessary for survival, alcohol is, therefore, considered by our warped brains to be a tool for survival. When we switch decision-making over to the amygdala— survival mode—our animal brains will seek alcohol without consultation of our logical conscious minds. Do you remember when I explained the many similar stories I have heard about alcoholics in early recovery finding themselves drinking with no recollection of attaining the alcohol? They were likely in a severe blood-sugar valley when this happens. It doesn't matter how committed they are to sobriety, or how strong their willpower is, when they spike their blood sugar with refined carbs and sugary treats, the resulting plummeting blood sugar leads to relapse.

Do you know what else our animal brains associate with survival when we have a blood-sugar plunge? Sugar and simple carbs, of course. When we give our bodies what our survival brains ask for, sugary, carb-loaded treats, the vicious cycle continues. Our blood sugar spikes, insulin is over-released dropping our blood sugar dangerously low, and we either drink alcohol or consume more sugar.

No wonder recovery is such a monumental challenge. We make it infinitely harder on ourselves by accepting the concept of harm reduction and allowing ourselves to eat all the sugar and carbs we want. We think we'll just address that much less dangerous sugar addiction transference later. Little did we know, until the brain chemistry research became conclusive in recent years, the sugar addiction is not less harmful than the alcohol addiction. It is the same addiction but fed by a different input. The likelihood of alcoholic relapse is revived by sugar or alcohol. Our amygdala really doesn't care and can hardly tell the difference.

When I lost 40 pounds on my diet of fat-free pretzels, fat-free cream cheese and vodka in the late 90s, I endured a strange new phenomenon. I often felt lightheaded and experienced sudden flashes of irritation. I chalked the sensation up to the weight loss, or the two rounds of cardio I was doing every day. I eventually learned to alleviate the sensation by eating a snack or drinking some alcohol, depending on the time of day, and thus, the drinking appropriateness. Ingesting food or alcohol would solve the problem and put the irritation and lightheadedness to rest.

Now that I understand the impact of nutrition on blood sugar and brain chemistry, the sensation I experienced while on a high-sugar, high-simple-carb and high-alcohol diet makes perfect sense. My lifestyle was driving my blood sugar to spike, and then to plummet. The lightheadedness and irritation were part of my entry into survival mode, and the transition of my decision-making from my prefrontal cortex to my amygdala. My animal brain was angry, and I needed to feed it to calm it down. The cycle repeated itself quite regularly while I was losing weight. I didn't know it at the time, but I was dramatically increasing my dependence on alcohol with every blood-sugar dive, and carb-y or boozy rescue mission.

Food Can Weaken Cravings

So, what's the solution? Cravings in early sobriety are serious business, and our willpower is no match for the power of the subconscious mind. As long as the subconscious considers alcohol to be essential for survival, the cravings feel earth-shatteringly intense. What can we do to lessen the temptation to relapse?

We are learning more and more about the power of food to prevent and cure many of the world's deadliest chronic diseases including diabetes, heart disease and cancer. And I have good news for you: the right food can decrease, and eventually eliminate, our cravings for alcohol making recovery from addiction much more realistic and attainable.

I have worked extensively with The Addiction Nutritionist, Kelly Miller, to understand these concepts and eat a diet that enhances my recovery. Kelly is doing amazing work in this area and helping thousands find freedom from addiction. For more information about Kelly, or to consult with her and receive nutrition advice specific to your needs, you can find her by searching The Addiction Nutritionist on social media, or at TheAddictionNutritionist.com.

To reduce our cravings for alcohol, we have to eat a diet that accomplishes two goals. First, the foods we eat need to help us balance our blood sugar and keep us out of the spike and plummet zone of survival mode. Second, we need to eat a variety of foods that promote the regeneration of our pleasure neurotransmitters.

Frankly, a nutrition plan that accomplishes those two goals is advisable not just for an alcoholic in recovery, but for everyone interested in mood improvement and neural homeostasis. Lots of pleasure neurotransmitters and balanced blood sugar should be universal human goals regardless of experience with addiction.

The standard American diet causes huge problems that go far beyond hindering recovery from alcoholism. Full of processed convenience foods high in sugar, simple carbs, chemicals and fillers, the diet most of us eat, and the major food companies promote, is quite literally killing us. Addiction, diabetes, heart disease or cancer—any of the above are coming for us when we are on the standard American diet. When we switch to eating a diet that promotes recovery from alcoholism, we also improve our chances of avoiding countless other chronic diseases.

The good news about eating the diet I'm about to describe is that, for most of us, it is mostly about addition with only two major food subtractions. You probably guessed it: added sugars and refined carbohydrates have got to go. If you had plans to adopt a fat-free pretzel, fat-free cream cheese and vodka diet with a side order of alcoholism, the recovery diet I'm about to describe will be a shock to your system.

The nutrition plan that helped me regenerate my pleasure neurotransmitters and balance my blood sugar comes down to filling my plate at mealtime with foods from three broad and delicious categories.

Half of my plate is a variety of vegetables grown above ground. Root vegetables are starchy and high in carbs and sugars. I still eat sweet potatoes, carrots, radishes and onions, but I limit my intake of those tubers. I focus instead on lettuce, celery, cabbage, broccoli, spinach, cauliflower, mushrooms, brussels sprouts, asparagus, squash and the dozens of other delicious veggies grown above ground. The nutrients available in the vegetables occupying half of my plate are vital to neurotransmitter regeneration. They are delicious, they look healthy and I know they are helping my brain to heal.

A quarter of my plate is occupied by fat and protein, largely from clean animal sources. This does not include antibiotic, preservative, sugar and chemical-laden fast food, but I do eat lots of meats and cheeses with clean labels. The proteins and fats serve two vital purposes to enhance recovery.

Animal proteins are our primary source for the amino acids that are absolutely necessary for generating new neurotransmitters. Without these amino acids, our bodies cannot make these vital pleasure chemicals. If you don't eat meat, amino acid supplements are an option, but the best, most natural sources for these critical amino acids are the meats in which they naturally occur.

Fats are necessary in our diet because the composition of our brain cells is almost 60 percent fat. It just makes simple, logical sense that we should eat fats if we want to help our brains to heal. If you want healthy brain cells, give your brain plenty of its main component. In addition to animal fats like meat and dairy, avocados, olive oils and nuts are excellent sources of healthy, natural brain-feeding fats.

The last quarter of my plate is made up of whole grain carbs and fruits. Carbohydrates have an important and healthy role in our diets. They just need to come from unrefined sources, and they need to be consumed in limited quantities. The same is true for fruits. They are full of vitamins and other nutrients. I certainly don't need to sell you on the healthiness of strawberries or oranges or bananas. But fruits are high in naturally occurring sugars, so we need to be mindful of keeping fruit consumption in check to keep our blood sugar in balance.

This is my ideal meal plan. It is neither complicated nor restrictive, and it leaves me with a wide variety of delicious options. When I am at home, this is how I eat. When I am traveling or eating out, however, balancing my plate like this is quite a bit more challenging. When on the road, I stick to one simple rule: I don't eat, or at least I severely limit, added sugars and refined carbs. If I'm at a cookout, I take my burger without the bun. When at a restaurant with friends, I try to get deep in conversation instead of deep into the bread or chips served before the entrée. It is simple, but not always easy. I try to keep the results in mind. Improved mood, and no cravings for alcohol, usually help me feel satisfied without ordering desert. Balancing my plate as described above is more difficult when away from home, but resisting added sugars and processed carbs is a simple and manageable restriction.

In addition to three meals, I also eat two snacks every day. I don't split my snacks between half this and a quarter that. That seems arduous and unmanageable to me. Instead, I just make sure my snacks do not include added sugars or simple carbs. A handful of mixed nuts or an apple with peanut butter are common snacks for me. Half an avocado or a wedge of some fancy cheese really hit the spot, too. When traveling, beef jerky often accompanies me on the trip.

And when I really need desert, dark chocolate with its low sugar content is quite satisfying. Dark chocolate covered almonds or walnuts make me wonder why I ever ate ice cream or cookies in the first place.

The snacks are really important and should not be missed. Keeping our blood sugar in balance is as critical a component to a recovery-friendly lifestyle as there is. Especially while our subconscious minds associate alcohol with survival, keeping our decision-making out of the amygdala is vital. I cannot overemphasize how important this is. Three meals and two snacks are critical to staying out of the survival-mode danger zone.

Have you ever heard that if you're thirsty, it's too late? If you are thirsty, you are already dehydrated. Try to think of eating in the same way, and don't let yourself get hungry. Eat reasonable portions of balanced foods at regular intervals, and you'll avoid letting your blood sugar drop too low.

When I first adopted this nutrition plan to aid in my recovery, I didn't understand this most important factor. When I wasn't hungry, I skipped snacks. When I was busy, I skipped meals. As long as I was distracted and not thinking about food, I didn't eat. I thought it was a good thing. I looked at it like calories saved. I'm always up for dropping a pound or two, so I thought I was doing the right thing by not eating whenever I was comfortable avoiding food.

Here's the thing: skipping meals or snacks lets our blood sugar drop too low. Even when I was well past the point of craving alcohol, when my animal brain was making decisions, I wasn't able to fight the cravings to overeat. The amygdala is put in charge when we are in survival mode. The amygdala is unfamiliar with the concept of portion control.

When I skipped a meal or snack, my animal brain had me eating like I hadn't seen food in days. I more than made up for the calories I conserved by skipping earlier in the day.

And the choices weren't the best, either. When I did gorge on sweets, it was always after skipping a meal. Eat when it is time to eat, not when you are hungry or have time. Prioritize food for your own health and happiness.

This is the nutrition plan that works for me. Generally speaking, and not taking your specific nutrient needs into consideration, it is a great place to start for anyone seeking to improve their chances for successful alcoholism recovery. If, however, you'd like a customized plan that takes all your specifics into account, I know my friend Kelly Miller, The Addiction Nutritionist, would be happy to hear from you.

What you eat can cure you, and it's really not that hard or restrictive. Until traditional methods of recovery incorporate the relationship between brain chemistry, blood sugar and nutrition into their programs, you now have knowledge that's dramatically underutilized in the addiction recovery community. This is another critical tool for your recovery toolbox with potential to do some serious building and nurturing of your sobriety muscles.

If you are an alcoholic in early recovery, I recommend you read chapters nine and ten repeatedly until you are really comfortable with the topics of brain chemistry and nutrition. This information isn't a neat little knowledge trinket you can use to accessorize your recovery. This stuff is fundamental and has the potential to be life changing.

If you are the loved one of an alcoholic, I have two messages for you. First, your knowledge of these most important subjects could potentially help you help the drinker you love. Second, this nutrition plan has benefits for you, too. After all, who doesn't want more pleasure neurotransmitters in their melon?

chapter 11 | building sobriety muscles

Nothing is more important in early sobriety than learning a naturally occurring degree of patience, something that's universally unavailable to serious drinkers. In active alcoholism, I used booze to accomplish a lot of different goals. Settling myself down was one the pillars of my alcohol consumption. In early sobriety, I had no idea how to be calm even for a few minutes, so patience was out of the question.

There are so many aspects to recovery from alcoholism that make the process complex and daunting. And the process takes time. A lot of time. In early sobriety I wanted my life to continue unchanged—except without a beer in my hand. I was so naive; it doesn't work that way. In sobriety from alcoholism, everything changes. Everything.

There are things we can do to help the process of recovery along though, and I'm sharing every tip I've learned through personal experience and the stories of so many other recovery warriors. But sometimes, time is the only healer. Don't think of recovery like a speedboat that you can whip in this direction or that. Think of recovery like a huge ocean-going vessel trying to turn around in a crowded bay. It takes precision, slow movements, some help from the tugboats and a whole lot of patience. If you want to change your life in such a fundamental way as removing that which has become your unfortunate first priority, you are going to have to wait for it.

Nobody has the misperception that sobriety is easy. What most people don't understand, however, is success takes a whole lot of time. But is there anything significant that you are good at that didn't require years of practice?

While my specific experiences described in this chapter
are about a drinker learning to battle through early sobriety,
the lesson of patience most definitely applies to the loved
ones of drinkers, too. Defense mechanisms, resentments,
anger, a lack of trust—all the emotions associated with loving
an alcoholic—require a lot of time and patience to heal.
There is nothing quick or easy about recovery from
alcoholism, for any of the victims.

Emotions: Where have you been all my life?

It is often said in the recovery community that we alcoholics
have the emotional maturity of the age when we started
drinking. Alcohol stunts our emotional growth because we
learn to use booze to medicate our feelings away. It is an
effective tool to wash away fear, longing, sadness, pain and
any other emotions that bring us discomfort. But chemically
suppressing our emotions is a far cry from dealing with them.
So the years and decades of learning to drink when we feel
bad is useless in sobriety.

When I stopped drinking, it was as if I was in my late
teens again learning how to behave like an adult in the face of
adversity. This is a difficult topic to process, especially for us
men, as society has taught us to limit our expression and
discussion of emotions. I most sincerely think this might be
the single greatest contributor to the fact that men still
outpace women in becoming addicted to alcohol. Damn our
culture! Society makes us alcoholics by convincing us that our
lives are incomplete without involving alcohol in every facet.
Even if we avoid that trap, society convinces us, especially
males, to push down painful emotions at all costs, then

reminds us of the perfect toxic tool to imbibe to do the job of emotional suppression.

Think about it for a minute. Which of these statements would confuse or alienate our friends if they heard us say them?

» I've been under a lot of stress at work. I need a drink!

» We've had a death in the family. My siblings and I are going to need a lot of whiskey to get through this one.

» My wife and I just had another fight. I'm going to the bar to cool off.

» I'm really sad and I don't know why. I just want to cry, and I don't know what to do to feel better.

The first three sound like normal, adult behavior. They might even receive a chuckle of understanding and commiseration from your friends. But the fourth statement would worry your friends, especially if you are a guy. It is the only one of these statements that represents healthy management of emotional discomfort. The last statement is how humans are supposed to behave. But that might lose you some friends and cause others to really worry about you.

Using alcohol to cover-up emotions, that's what should be worrying. Hiding behind booze makes us emotionally weak and unstable. Which of those four statements does society mistakenly associate with weakness? Drinking is tough. Chasing pain with whiskey is manly and rugged. Do you understand how wrong that is? This is not a minor point. Not crying is a sign of weakness. Being emotionally inept makes us incomplete humans incapable of certain necessary interactions with the important people in our lives.

Are your relationships a hot mess? Maybe you are in
early sobriety, and you place all the blame for the dysfunction
on your behavior when drinking. I believe you when you and
the people you love report that you acted like an asshole
when you drank. But that's only part of the story. By being so
emotionally stunted, you also wrecked your relationships
because you can't manage feelings, your feelings and those of
the people you love, like an adult. Not the socially approved
picture of adulthood, sulking with a glass of poison in your
hand. The kind of adult we were designed to be—staring
sadness, anger, hurt and frustration in the eye and trying like
hell not to blink. That's emotional maturity. If you're like I
was, you've got a ton of growing up to do.

There is a lot of "work" to do in recovery. There is a ton
of learning, personal discovery, brain chemistry repair,
relationship salvaging and so on. But the work of emotional
maturity is much less about work, and more about patience.
There's nothing you can do to speed up or simplify learning
how to feel all your feelings without poisoning them away. It
just happens. No real, assertive work, except don't drink. As
long as you don't make the mistake of transferring your
addiction to alcohol to another addictive substance or activity
with similar neurochemistry hijacking power, the emotional
maturity will just happen over time. Over a long, long period
of time. This is where the need for patience becomes critical.

Being sad is part of the human condition. Sadness comes
and goes based on things happening around us, and
sometimes, for no tangible reason at all. Learning to sit with
our sadness is a huge component of the emotional maturity
of recovery. Years into my permanent sobriety, I was still
grappling with the waves of emotions that rolled over me,
ready or not. I've now reached a point where I kind of

welcome the sadness when it comes. I know it will be
grounding, it will force me to be introspective, it puts me in a
spiritual zone—and it will depart as unexpectedly as it came,
being replaced by whatever emotion is next on the feelings
roller-coaster.

Nothing lasts forever: not joy, not sadness, not
excitement, not frustration and not pain. We feel the feels
because that's how we were designed. It is a sign of a properly
functioning cranial unit. So many people mistake normal
human sadness for clinical depression. There is a difference
that I'm not qualified to explain. What I know for sure,
however, is that our societal fixation with happiness is
unhealthy and unrealistic. I also know that the sadness makes
me appreciate the joy when it comes, now more than ever
before.

Confidence Grows from Patience

I was about two weeks sober and feeling good about my
decision. My determination to leave my drinking life behind
was strong, and I was starting to see some fledgling little
benefits to sobriety. But there was nothing patient about my
approach to recovery. I wanted to be fixed, and I wanted it
immediately. I'm going to share a story I briefly mentioned in
chapter three, but here I'll tell you all the impatient details.

I was tossing a ball back and forth with one of my sons in
our backyard when my neighbor yelled over the fence. "Hey
Matt! Do you want to go to the Rockies game tonight? I've
got an extra ticket." My neighbor, Mike, was as nice a guy as I
knew. He owned a very successful business, and he had a lot
of friends. He was constantly entertaining, and heavy drinking

was always involved. I was often honored to be invited to join him and his gang of drinking buddies.

I froze for a second as I considered his invitation. He had no idea I'd stopped drinking, and there would surely be questions. But I was determined not to let a little thing like sobriety interrupt my life. I would attend the Major League Baseball game just as I'd done lots of times before. The only difference was, this time, I'd do it without a drink in my hand. I was strong. I was confident. I gratefully accepted my neighbor's invitation. In fact, I offered to be the designated driver.

I thought I was being bold and embracing my new sobriety. What I didn't understand was that I set myself up for one of the most miserable experiences of my life.

Mike and his friends brought "roadies" in the car for the drive to Coors Field, and they clearly weren't their first beverages of the day. When we arrived at the ballpark, I was not surprised to learn that Mike had club-level seats. The club level is that sliver of rows between the lower deck and the upper deck with private entrances to keep out the riffraff. The view of the playing field is alright. The fans in the lower deck are much closer to the action.

But the view isn't the point, really. Club-level fans have access to sushi and steak and fancy desserts not available on the lower or upper deck where hotdogs and peanuts are the most popular fare. The club level has another bonus, the one that probably attracts most of the high rollers to the tickets despite the increased ticket price. It's the perk that explains why Mike sprung for the club level for sure. The club level had a full bar including top-shelf liquors. Mike and his friends weren't going to swill warm beers from plastic cups in front of me. They hit the whiskey on the rocks and gin and tonics that night, and they hit them hard.

As a drinker in early sobriety, I felt naked sitting there without a drink in my hand. As Mike and his friends downed round after round, the volume of the conversation increased at the same rate that my interest in the stories being scream-told decreased. I was sure everyone else on the club level was looking my way and wondering what was the matter with me, and why was I drinking water. Didn't I know I was at a baseball game and I was supposed to be having fun? I was with the rowdiest group on our side of the stadium. I felt like a dweeby loser encased in a gaggle of cool kids.

I could feel the eyes of a hundred people staring at me with pity for my pathetic teetotaling disgracefulness. As the night wore on, Mike and his friends became less and less tolerant of my decision to abstain. "Come on man. Have a drink. What's the matter with you?" When the game ended and we walked the concourse toward my car, Mike almost got in a fight with another well-lubricated fan over the brand of beer he was drinking. They had a third-grade level shouting match over the superiority of Budweiser versus Miller Lite (at Coors Field, no less). I would have not believed it had I not seen it with my own eyes. Except, of course I would have believed it. If I had been drinking, instead of looking on in shameful disgust, I would have picked a side and emphatically hurled slurred insults.

I made two critical mistakes that night. The second mistake was agreeing to be the designated driver to a bunch of drinkers while I was in early sobriety. One of the most important lessons I've learned from others in recovery is to always have a planned exit strategy when entering a boozy environment when newly sober. Don't accept a ride to the party from others, and don't offer to give rides, either. Make it as easy as possible to ditch without saying goodbye. Climb out a bathroom window if you must. When the urge to drink comes in early sobriety, it can be overwhelming in an instant. Protect yourself and your sobriety by being selfish, especially when it comes to transportation in your first year or more sober.

The first critical mistake I made would have made mistake number two irrelevant had I not made it in the first place. Confused? Let me clear it up for you. Don't socialize in environments that include alcohol in early sobriety. Period. Had I not thought myself tough and put myself in that alcoholic situation, I would not have experienced the trauma of that baseball game, and I would not have had to stay to the end to drive the drunk bus.

It doesn't matter how strong you are. Your determination and willpower are not the point. The point is that you are neurologically injured, and your condition needs time to heal. Jumping naked into the fire doesn't help anything. Protect your sobriety. Cancel your social life until your subconscious mind heals. The tough might white-knuckle through one bad experience or another, but the smart lay low until they have the advantage of time. Patience leads to victory over the beast that is alcoholism.

I didn't drink that night at the baseball game. I made it home and collapsed under the weight of misperception and temptation. I felt worse about myself than ever before in my life. There was no satisfaction in sobriety. I was ashamed of my alcoholism, and even more ashamed of my sobriety when surrounded by drinkers. I felt absolutely worthless.

I didn't drink that night, but my brain and body were filled with weakness, and all the confidence I had built in my couple of weeks of sobriety was replaced with paralyzing doubt.

I didn't drink that night, but within a week, I was back to drinking away the pain, and digging my pit of alcoholic despair. Alcoholism is deadly serious business, and the disease doesn't care how tough you think you are. There are so many aspects of recovery that rely, absolutely 100 percent depend, on your ability to be patient. Your sobriety muscles will grow, and you don't really have to do anything to make that happen. In fact, doing nothing is exactly the way to make yourself stronger.

Plan Your Year of Healing

Get out your calendar, and look week by week, day by day, for a whole year into the future. If you are in your first year of sobriety, make a list of all the events that you know you will, or think you will, be invited to attend that will feature alcohol. The list might include annual family traditions, neighborhood cookouts, work functions, planned vacations and holiday parties. Take your time and be thorough.

Now circle only the events on the list that you absolutely, positively cannot miss. There should be very few circled items. The only things that deserve to be circled include truly important work functions that will get you fired if you don't attend, and family traditions that you really cannot miss. Just because you've done it for years, or you're afraid of losing your friends if you miss, is not reason enough to circle these events.

On my list, there were only three things circled: Christmas with my parents at our house, a week in the summer in South Carolina with family and the Indianapolis 500 in May with friends and my wife's family. Notice, every one of my three included close family. Family needs us, and we need them. If they are supportive of our recovery, a few events with family deserve circles. The Indy 500 was risky for me, but it was a 30+ year tradition, and the tickets were very expensive. I had to be there, or our host would have eaten the cost of my family's six tickets. I know he would not have accepted money from me had we not attended, so this one was quite tricky to navigate.

I came up with an exit plan, prepared for white-knuckling and circled that event. Even with all that justification, looking back now, that circle was probably a mistake, and it could have cost me my sobriety.

All the rest of the un-circled events left on your list are canceled for the year. Please cross them out. It will be tough. In the case of some events with close friends that were your favorites of the year as a drinker, it will be excruciating to take a pass. But your long-term sobriety, hell, your whole future, depends on having the strength to let your patience grow your sobriety muscles.

Crossing the un-circled events off your list for one year will ensure your ability to safely attend all events you choose in future years. My sobriety muscles are strong enough now to easily attend any boozy event without temptations or discomfort. In permanent sobriety, I've found I don't enjoy many of the drunk fests that used to line my calendar, but it is not a question of staying sober. It is a question of dealing with drunks in an otherwise boring environment. There are lots of situations that I can easily put myself in now, but I choose not to because I've wasted enough time.

I spent 10 years trying to get sober. That is 10 years of quitting drinking, then relapsing, because I thought I was stronger than the beast of alcoholism. I wasted 10 years trying to prove that willpower and determination was enough. If 10 years of failure taught me nothing else, the lesson is that patience is far more effective than resolve.

Patience means accepting that early sobriety lasts a year or more. Patience means embracing that the part of your brain that you don't control is far more powerful than the part you do. Patience means making excuses, lying if you have to, to avoid putting your healing brain in threatening situations, no matter how tough you think you are. Patience means success in recovery. There are no shortcuts.

If sobriety was easy, a whole lot more people would successfully do it. Recovery is diabolically hard because it requires a talent that alcoholics universally lack. Sitting, waiting, feeling, healing and growing into emotional maturity, without the aid of our 80-proof elixir, will be one of the greatest challenges of our lives. Impatience makes the task impossible.

But as challenging as it is, permanent sobriety is so worth it. Emotional maturity is a possession all grown adults deserve. Shameless comfort in any situation without regard to the existence or absence of booze is a liberating freedom. You'll get there, if only you find the strength to admit your weakness and wait for your sobriety muscles to grow.

chapter 12 | the power of vulnerability

As I walked in the door, my wife, Sheri, said, "You need to call my nephew. I don't know what's wrong, but he doesn't sound good. He called asking for you."

Stephen has been one of my favorite relatives since, at age 10, he helped Sheri and me move to St. Paul, Minnesota right after college. We had a lot of fun on that trip, de-pantsing each other in public and trying to muscle-down pizza slices covered in about an inch of crushed red pepper. He was such a sweet kid, always with a smile on his face and a story he was eager to tell. We live a thousand miles apart now, and we only see each other once a year. But I've felt a connection to Stephen ever since we laughed our way across the Midwest in the summer of 1995.

There was no laughter in his voice when he answered my return call. Alcohol can suck the joy out of anyone. The innocence of the week I spent with Stephen, age 10, was long gone. Since then, I had let alcohol squeeze all the fun out of my life. I had battled addiction for 10 years, and finally found permanent sobriety. Now, my beloved nephew was reaching out for help.

Until I announced my alcoholism and my recovery, in the most public way I could find, Stephen had no idea that I was suffering. He just looked at me like his happy Uncle Matt who came to town for a week every summer and drank beer while grilling hotdogs and playing kickball. That's exactly how it works, high-functioning alcoholism. Nothing to see here! Everything's fine. Grab me another beer from the cooler while I tend to the grill. Save some potato salad for me. Had I not eventually told everybody about the demon that lurked

below the surface, slowly killing me and destroying my life, he
would not have known that the guy with whom he shared the
grilling tongs was an alcoholic. Had he not known he never
would have made that phone call.

Stephen and I talked for a long time that day. In the days,
weeks and months that followed, we talked and texted quite
regularly as he figured out the plan for recovery that made
the most sense for him. Eventually, he didn't need my
support anymore. We've gone back to seeing each other
once a year, and only talking or texting occasionally. But the
bond I felt for my beloved nephew grew unbreakably strong
that day because of that one desperate phone call—a call he
never would have made if he never would have known.

Our Secrets Protect the Disease

Anonymity is selfish. Alcoholism is one of the most
stigmatized conditions in the world, and our reluctance to
talk about it is killing people.

I understand the argument for anonymity, and it makes
sense, really. Unless we promise to protect the identity of
people who suspect their drinking has become a problem,
they wouldn't even consider seeking help. It's the same
reason that so many in the alcoholism recovery community
refuse to call themselves alcoholics. They are afraid that the
people who need help will compare themselves to the
toothless drunks living under bridges. Since they are not,
"that bad," they must not be alcoholics, and thus, must not
need help.

So, avoiding the word, "alcoholic," and promising
anonymity for anyone who walks into the rooms, are
philosophies based in logic. But they are wrong. Dead wrong.

It is like arguing that the end justifies the means. It doesn't. Speaking the truth and expecting our audience to be adult enough to handle it, is the only way to end the stigma that's killing people. A stigma that has over 15 million Americans trapped in alcohol dependency.

We've tried anonymity. We've tried avoiding the diagnosis. What has resulted is an epidemic that's growing, not shrinking. Alcoholism is a societal problem. When we promote alcohol as necessary to celebrate, mourn, relax, party and relieve stress, we encourage people to become addicted. And when we keep the negative consequences as a secret only told in church basements and hushed whispers, we don't do the epidemic of alcoholism the justice that will be required to reverse the trend. What do you think happened when the Marlboro Man sat handsomely puffing away atop his horse before it was widely known that smoking causes cancer? Everyone smoked. It was a no-brainer, right? But when the direct link between smoking and death became widely accepted, smoking didn't look quite as appealing, no matter what the studly cowboy portrayed.

We can end the stigma, and we can cure the scourge of alcoholism. We don't need any new scientific research to do that. The World Health Organization calculates that over three million people die each year to alcohol-related causes. That number's plenty large and unacceptable. We just need to spread the word. We need people to understand and know about alcohol-induced depression. We need the world to know about destroyed relationships, lost jobs and the deterioration of health, both mental and physical. We don't need to tell the people in the rooms of AA about all of this. They already know.

If we want to make a difference, we need the rest of the world to know, too.

Recovering Out Loud

Being open about my recovery is the single biggest factor in the success of my sobriety. I love helping people. I love working to defeat the stigma. I love that my story gives others, like my nephew, the strength to change their lives. All that feels wonderful, but those are all by-products of the real reason I recover out loud. I am open about my recovery because I'm selfish.

All humans are self-centered to varying degrees. A primary concern for our own well-being is a form of preservation. It's not always bad to be selfish. In some ways, it is necessary for survival. And that statement most definitely applies to the way I selfishly protect my sobriety by being open about my alcoholism. Confused much? Let me explain.

Recovering out loud keeps me sober in two critical ways that elude people who keep their alcoholic secrets a secret. First, my admission of human weakness and repentance has allowed me to develop many deep and meaningful relationships with other people that would not have been available to me had I remained silent. It is widely accepted that we are all secretly dealing with issues beyond the knowledge of the people around us. Having serious problems is part of the human condition and keeping our shit a secret is a socially accepted best practice. So, what happens when we talk about our stuff publicly, with, and in front of, other people?

The other people feel a kinship with us. They admire our vulnerability, and they empathize with our plight. And our

thing doesn't need to be their thing for this bond to form. I
have developed close relationships with people with eating
disorders, porn addictions, histories of being abused and
recent financial collapses. The details aren't important. What
changes relationships is my willingness to expose my
weaknesses. By owning my alcoholic label, and sharing what
I've learned about recovery, I give others permission to be
vulnerable, too.

And even the people in my life who struggle to find their
voice feel closer to me because I've found mine. I have many
relationships where a bond is clearly there, and I don't know
the first thing about their traumatic stories. Vulnerability is
not easy, but it is powerful. In many cases, my vulnerability is
powerful enough for the both of us.

Connection is so important to contentment and
happiness. I've always had a lot of friends. What I didn't
understand, until I opened up about my alcoholism, is how
few truly connected relationships I had. Now that I am loud
and proud, so many acquaintances have turned into close
friendships. Many friends have become soul mates of sorts. A
nod and a wave have turned into a hug and a mutual
knowing. The connection is powerful. It is born from
perseverance through a shared experience, even when the
details of the experience are vastly different. It is knowing that
I've struggled, and you've struggled, too, and that makes us
both inextricably linked survivors.

The second reason I am selfishly served by recovering
out loud is quite a bit more basic and externally accessible.
My openness about my addiction means I can never drink
again. My friends aren't social deviants or depraved criminals.
They are the kind of upstanding citizens and contributors to
society with which you would expect a high-functioning

alcoholic to associate. If I ever tried to drink with them again, after all the trauma and turmoil I have revealed, they would reject me and physically remove the alcohol from my possession. They can't unknow the details I've shared with them. As a result, they will never drink with me again.

And it goes much deeper than that. I would have to get a new job, move to a different part of the country and start a new family if I ever started drinking again. That's if I survived the getaway, that is. My wife and I have joked on several occasions that if I tried to pick the bottle back up, there would likely be some combination of murder/suicide in our bedroom. Suicide is no laughing matter. Nor is murder. They aren't funny, but they are realistic likelihoods from any ill-fated attempt to drink alcohol again on my part.

As a high-functioning alcoholic who kept my destruction under wraps, my alcohol-induced transgressions have been largely forgiven or overlooked by my community, just as quickly as I described them. If I was to ever start drinking again, however, the details of those stories would be used against me to predict an inevitable future that would include my employment termination and exile to a place where the drunks live. Under a bridge or into a gutter, perhaps. It would be over if I drank. It would all be over.

I cherish hearing how my story of recovery has helped others find their paths to freedom from alcohol. And I'm not just talking about the recovery stories of people I love. It is almost as rewarding to hear from strangers that my willingness to be vulnerable has touched them and given them permission to seek help. I wish I was generous or compassionate enough for that to be the reason I recover out loud. But it is not.

I recover out loud because it leads to deep and meaningful relationships, and it solidifies my sobriety. Alcoholism is a disease of selfishness. Some of the selfishness carries over into recovery, I guess. The benefits I gain through my selfish determination to be open in my recovery don't fill me with shame and regret. Recovering out loud is an undeniable upgrade to the private terror of alcoholism.

Coming Out

All this talk of open recovery is great, in theory. The personal benefits are surpassed only by the potential to eliminate the stigma associated with alcoholism. There is just one problem. The idea of sharing my secret alcoholism with anyone, let alone everyone, was paralyzingly terrifying for me in early sobriety. My wife, my parents, my sister, my mother-in-law and my sister-in-law were the only humans on earth that knew how much trouble I was in. The idea of increasing my inner circle by even one additional person was completely unthinkable.

I loved drinking socially, but I did most of my serious drinking at home. I played soccer in an adult men's league on Thursday nights. After the matches, my teammates and I made a habit of washing down victory or washing away defeat in the pub attached to the sports center. I had a few beers with my boys, then went home and drank thirstily before stumbling to bed. I never overdid it in front of my drinking buddies.

There were social occasions when I did drink too much and get noticeably drunk. Those indiscretions were so rare, and mostly with different sets of friends each of the few times it happened, that it just appeared I had overdone it as a one-

off, not as part of any discernible pattern. "Boy, were you
drunk last weekend. I've never seen you like that, but I've
been there before myself," was the most likely reaction I
would occasionally receive from friends.

I didn't miss work, I kept my yard manicured and my
finances intact. From the outside, my marriage was as
enviable as my personality was outgoing. There just really
didn't seem to be a problem. And I worked hard to keep up
those appearances. Alone in my basement, in front of a
basketball game or movie I was pretending to watch—that's
where I did my serious drinking. That's where my alcoholism
was undeniably clear, and only my wife had to witness that
horror.

So in early sobriety, I had no interest in blowing the lid
off the secret I'd spent decades protecting. I was so full of
shame, and I couldn't imagine sharing my embarrassing
truth. I was ashamed of the alcoholic I had become, and
equally ashamed to be a fun-less, teetotaling loser. Even in
recovery early on, I held alcohol in such high esteem. I did
not yet see it for the poison it truly is. I viewed alcohol as the
bastion of success and maturity and viewed myself as cursed
for being allergic to it.

I learned a lot in my first year of sobriety. I learned all the
things I've shared here in the preceding chapters about brain
chemistry, bibliotherapy, nutrition, patience, emotions,
sobriety muscles and correctly identifying alcohol as a poison
in any quantity. When I knew it—when I truly believed the
aspects of my disease that I've shared here with you—I was
ready to share it all with the world. So one year into my
permanent sobriety, I started working on my plan for coming
out as an alcoholic.

I started counting all the email addresses I had in my possession. I had business cards from over two decades of adulthood in a couple of different careers, lots of personal connections and the email list associated with our small business. I decided to send a "coming out" letter to each person who had ever given me their email address. No screening. No filtering out to avoid particular embarrassment. I had a side gig as a high school soccer coach, and I even planned to send the letter to my athletic director despite my debilitating fear of being fired.

The fear of termination for being an alcoholic in recovery is as common as it is irrational. Think about it for a minute: I was going to tell my boss that I'd previously had a problem that I had now resolved. I was preparing to tell him that I was less likely than just about anyone else who worked for him to drink alcohol and cause an embarrassment for the school. I, the sober one, was terrified that he'd fire me. I'd done nothing illegal. I had no baggage that could impact my job, my school or the district. I was owning my disease and explaining my cure, and yet, I was convinced I would no longer be welcome at the job I so loved.

Why did this fear top my list of terror as I planned to send this letter? Because it is a huge part of the stigma. Alcoholism is a dirty word, and to tarnish myself in such a way was to declare myself unfit for humanity. That's how I felt, and there was no convincing me otherwise. I was absolutely sure I would be fired for beating a chronic disease and getting healthy.

When it came to crafting the letter I would send, I had one very specific goal in mind: I wanted as many people as possible to open and read it. I had no interest in spending a lot of time pouring out my heart and revealing my darkest secrets to the unopened trash folder in the email accounts of my recipients. I knew some key points about the task at hand from my email marketing experience with our business. I knew the subject line needed to be borderline clickbait, I knew I needed to build suspense with the opening paragraph, and I knew vulnerability would be rewarded with readership. I was beginning the behind-the-scenes work on my SoberAndUnashamed.com blog at the time, and I was blessed to have hired the best possible writing coach for a personal narrative or memoir, Shari Caudron. She helped me immensely to craft exactly the message I wanted my letter to deliver. We spent hours drafting and revising until we were ready to unleash my story on the world. If you'd like to read my coming out letter in all its originally sent glory, please check it out at SoberAndUnashamed.com/coming-out-alcoholic.

When I was finished amassing my list, I had over 3,000 email addresses. All that was left was choosing a subject line. I wanted to take advantage of the shock factor, what with no one suspecting my addiction and all. I chose, "Coming Out," as the subject line because I felt it was ripe with intrigue and would result in the highest possible number of email openings, even from people who had long since forgotten who I was or why they'd given me a business card.

I wasn't a fan of social media, but I created Facebook, Instagram and Twitter accounts just to help me reach friends and distant family with my announcement. I was going to go big or go home. I had no interest in having hundreds of painful discussions about why I wasn't drinking at this barbeque or that family reunion over the next decade or so. I wanted to rip the shameful silence of my recovery off like a Band-Aid.

In preparation for pressing the send button, I thought often about what responses I expected. Certainly, I anticipated a great deal of support from friends and family who I loved. I expected a little bit of negativity from drinking buddies, or people who thought they drank a lot more than me and assumed I was exaggerating my problem. I was prepared for a lot of good, a little bad, and to be fired on the spot from the job I so loved.

I didn't sleep much for the nights leading up to the execution of my multifaceted communication plan that featured the sending of one very revealing letter a whole bunch of times. On the night of January 9, 2018, I didn't sleep at all. I didn't even try, really. I laid in bed next to my wife and prayed that I wasn't making a huge, life-destroying mistake and jeopardizing the well-being of my family. At 3 a.m., on January 10th, I launched my email and social media tactical plan, and with it, my reputation.

The resulting feedback greatly exceeded my anticipation. I did receive the support I thought I would get—I just got way more of it than I expected, and from people I didn't even know from around the globe. I received none of the negative results for which I prepared. In fact, some of my drinking buddies, while surprised and slightly disappointed to lose my cash when it was time to pay the tab, were among the most supportive of my decision to seek health for me and my family. The real magic was the depth of the relationships that my coming out letter allowed me to forge with the most unexpected of acquaintances. I've explained that phenomenon in great detail earlier in this chapter. It was one of the truly shocking joys of my lifetime.

Also, I didn't get fired. Not even close. My athletic director had plenty of issues to occupy his workdays. What I sent him was a solution. Not only did he not have a problem with my recovery, based on a conversation I had with him a year later, he didn't even remember I had sent the letter. Funny how we all have too many of our own problems with which to deal to be bothered with the problems of others.

I think often about what I would choose as the best day of my life. I am married and attended the births of our four kids. Those five days are obvious choices. In the opinions of many in alcoholism recovery, the first day of my permanent sobriety is a valid candidate as well. While those were all glorious, life-changing experiences for me, the most impactful day I've ever experienced was January 10th, 2018—the day I came out as an alcoholic.

If you are newly sober, and this story sounds both terrifying and not worth a second of your personal consideration, you are right where you should be. You are right where I was when I was trying to get sober, too.

It is widely agreed, within the alcoholism recovery community, that sobriety isn't the opposite of addiction. Connection is. I've learned through years of working with others that connection is absolutely critical to any serious attempt at sobriety. Connection can be found through bibliotherapy, and connection can be found with our closest of family or friends. But it can also be found by letting people in on our secret, little by little. Meaningful connections exist by expanding our inner circle ever-so-slightly, bit by bit. I've learned that my vulnerability has been rewarded every single time.

But after some time passes, maybe a year or so in recovery, and your sobriety muscles have grown, maybe then you won't think my coming out letter to be quite so crazy or drastic. Maybe you'll be ready to rip off your Band-Aid and secure your sobriety. Maybe you'll be selfish enough for freedom.

And maybe you'll be ready to welcome a very unexpected, potentially life-changing phone call from someone you love.

If you are a drinker in early sobriety, you have a story to tell for both selfish, and selfless reasons. If you love an alcoholic, your story is just as important, both for your personal strength and healing, and to connect to others and give them permission to connect with you.

The stigma thrives on secrets and silence. Nothing will be of more benefit to your recovery, if you are an alcoholic, or if you love an alcoholic, than working to destigmatize this dreadful disease. Your story will have a serious impact. Your healing awaits.

If you'd like to work with us to navigate your healing, to find your soberevolution, please consider joining us at SHOUTSobriety.com.

recovering a marriage

Part Three

chapter 13 | almost tragic

When I was drinking, I was absolutely, 100 percent certain that alcohol was not the cause of the problems in our marriage. Alcohol could not possibly have been to blame. If I allowed even a sliver of doubt to creep in, if I gave even a momentary nod to the possibility that alcohol was the source of the damage, I would have had to quit. This is a great example of how, with this disease of denial, we alcoholics are lying to ourselves as much as we are deceiving our loved ones.

When I did stop drinking, I was absolutely, 100 percent certain that alcohol was the cause of all the problems in our marriage. In early sobriety, I was laser focused on beating temptation and abstaining from alcohol. I thought that if I accomplished the goal of continued sobriety, all of our relationship problems would vanish and my wife would run eagerly into my arms, full of gratitude for my sacrifice and abundant bliss for the promise of our future together.

In both of those beliefs, I was unwavering in my conviction that I had it right. In both of those cases, I could not have been more wrong.

Sobriety Doesn't Fix Anything

My wife, Sheri, knew the truth all along. When I was drinking, she understood that the knot my addiction was tying for both of us wouldn't be easily undone. When I stopped drinking, it was more terrifying than relieving for Sheri. She was used to the devil she knew. She had built defense mechanisms, learned to read all the uncomfortable signs of my various levels of inebriation and developed a strong loathing for every cell in my body. Sobriety was the unknown. Not only would it not fix anything, but she would have to learn a new way for us to coexist. Both in active alcoholism and in sobriety, I was always looking for a way to rekindle our romance and have a "normal," less tension-filled marriage. I wanted an intimate spark, but I also wanted peace and contentment. I wanted conversations about groceries or the lawn or the kids or work to not end in frustration or anger. I wanted smiles and hugs and partnership.

Sheri, on the other hand, wanted to make it another day without killing me or packing up the kids and heading back home to her mother's house. She wanted all the stuff I wanted too, but she had a much firmer grasp on how close we were to making the 10 o'clock news or at least needing lawyers, than I did. I thought we were almost okay. She knew we were almost tragic.

Sheri and I spent the Sunday night of a Labor Day weekend at the Stanley Hotel in Estes Park, Colorado. The Stanley is the property that inspired the Overlook Hotel in the movie, The Shining. I was about eight months into my sobriety, we were alone for the night without the kids and my intentions were set on romance. Sheri's mindset was more in line with the marital relationship of the movie characters played by Jack Nicholson and Shelley Duvall.

Just minutes after we checked in and found our room, I was sprawled out naked on the bed. We had been hiking all day, so I pretended I just wanted to cool off and enjoy the mountain breeze coming through our open window. In truth, I was hoping for a little afternoon delight before we explored the town and looked for a restaurant for dinner.

As the day had progressed, and check-in time loomed, the anticipation had been building in both of us. For me, the time alone was so rare, and I was eager to see if we could get a noise complaint before the sunset. For Sheri, the idea of spending so much time alone with me was terrorizing. She knew where my mind was, and she had too much unresolved conflict swimming around in her head to even dream of romance. I thought I was being sexy, laying naked on the bed. For Sheri, the very sight of me, clothed or not, was repulsive.

Our clashing attitudes and intentions eventually became obvious, even to Captain Oblivious rolling around in my birthday suit. We did get it on, but not in the way I had in mind. We talked. For hours we discussed subjects both directly and indirectly related to our relationship. We didn't argue, we both remained calm and I joined my wife in her feelings of disappointment and uncertainty for the future. She was disappointed because of the mess alcoholism made of our lives, and I was disappointed because I was the only naked person in the room.

Our hours of talking that afternoon didn't really solve anything. We were both still too early in recovery to know how to address the pain, and too naive to understand the work we still needed to do. But the divide between us got a little narrower that day. Our heavy, tearful, empathetic afternoon conversation turned into a relief-filled, joyful dinner conversation. When we got back to the room, we didn't burn the hotel down with our passion as I had hoped, but we made tender love and slept soundly as if a burden had been lifted from both of us.

Sobriety didn't fix anything, but our mutual effort allowed us to make progress. I wish I could say it was a wake-up call for me about the road and the work ahead. It was not. I still didn't understand what would be required to recover our relationship. Sheri didn't either. All we knew at that moment was that for once in our marriage, without the distraction and destruction of alcohol, we made a lasting memory that was good—instead of adding another brick to the wall of resentment.

On our walk to dinner that night, we stood about 50 feet from a full-grown adult male elk. That was the good memory. You didn't think I was talking about the sex, did you?

The Selfishness of Early Sobriety

Sheri was accustomed to her and the kids being the second priority in my life. When in active alcoholism, I never would have admitted that my beloved IPA and whiskey on the rocks took precedence over my family. I wouldn't have admitted it because I didn't believe it. But it was true, and by my actions, I proved time and again that drinking alcohol was the shameful top priority in my life.

From my perspective, when I quit drinking, everything about my life changed. My routines were different, my enthusiasm and determination for sobriety were palpable, and I no longer trod the hardwood floors of our little bungalow like a half-conscious zombie. Even as I struggled, and even as my confidence waned, I was still a much better version of myself. And I was sure my wife could see that.

What Sheri could see in her reality was very different from the portrait I thought I was painting. I was still selfish and self-centered as I focused on getting and staying sober. It was still all about me: my pain, my temptations, my effort, my triggers and my endless need for support. On a conscious,

rational level, Sheri was all in. She knew how tenuous my
sobriety was, and she knew my health depended on my
success.

But she was still the second most important thing in my
life, now taking a back seat to my dedication to pursue
sobriety. On an emotional level, that still sucked.

I had apologized for the mean, careless, thoughtless and
hateful things I did in active alcoholism. I had apologized
early and often, and in a most sincere way. What I didn't
understand was that those apologies, made while alcohol was
still a part of my life, were useless. Because I was still a
drinker, my vile actions were guaranteed to be repeated in
the future, so the apologies, no matter how sincere, did not
land. Sheri could hardly stand still to listen to them. It was as
though I was apologizing for eating her second to last slice of
pizza, as I reached for her last slice of pizza.

So, while I was in early sobriety and was focused solely on
my health and my recovery, I ignored Sheri's needs because I
didn't think she had any. The idea that she had resentments
to work through didn't register for me. I had apologized for
all the bad stuff I did. I apologized the next day, and I
apologized in a general sense many times after. In my mind,
those issues were resolved cases of jackassery. I had put them
behind me. I assumed Sheri had done the same.

She had not. And dealing with the resentments was just
one of the ways Sheri needed to heal and recover from my
alcoholism. As long as I remained selfish and needy in my
fixation on my own recovery, and I gave no recognition to the
need for her to have resources and support to find healing
herself, I was still doing damage to our relationship.

There was some degree of necessity to the singular focus on my recovery. As an alcoholic trying to quit drinking, I faced cravings, triggers, temptations and a subconscious mind that was working against me. There was a sense of urgency to the task I was trying to accomplish. Success required focus, effort to learn, and support from my wife. My selfishness was not without merit, in a way. If we had not both made significant effort in getting me sober, I would have gone back to drinking. It had happened for the 10 previous years, over and over again, so it wasn't hard to imagine me relapsing.

Okay, so the selfishness is justified. Success depends on it. That doesn't prevent the selfishness from draining the life out of the loved ones of the alcoholic. Relationships thrive on give and take. Today we'll deal with my issue, and tomorrow we'll deal with yours. When it's the same person, day after day, getting all the frosting spread on his cupcake, the other person's cupcake gets pretty dry and crusty. It might be the right thing to do, but it still sucks.

I was a full year into my sobriety before I recognized Sheri's need to recover at all. I still didn't know what that meant but I was growing increasingly aware that my sobriety wasn't fixing anything, and Sheri had some work to do, too.

This awareness in and of itself was huge. It helped me see that I wasn't the only one hurting, and that my fixation on myself was selfish, and would eventually need to change.

Don't Drop Your Guard

When I talk about Sheri's semi-reluctant, but completely necessary, support of my efforts in early sobriety, her efforts were largely passive in nature. She gave me the time I needed, each and every night, to sit quietly and read about

alcoholism. She listened quietly, nodding her head and
making an occasional comment, as I talked incessantly about
brain chemistry, emotions, nutrition, patience and cravings to
drink. And she acquiesced, with only minimal resistance, to
my decision to avoid socializing for the first year of my
sobriety. Those were her friends, too, and for the most part,
she hermited down right alongside me.

All the while she supported my recovery and helped me
in innumerable ways, Sheri could not allow herself to be
convinced that sobriety was a solution. She hated the devil
she knew, but she'd learned to deal with me as a drinker. She
didn't know how much damage two-and-a-half decades of
heavy drinking had done to me, and she was nervous to find
out what kind of person her permanently sober husband
would turn out to be. Unlike me, who was convinced I'd be a
real gem once alcohol free, Sheri was afraid I would change
from a drunk asshole to a sober asshole.

She also didn't know if my commitment to sobriety
would stick. I'd made it to six months twice, and to nine
months of sobriety once. Why would Sheri believe this time
would be any different; months of resolve, followed by a
polishing of my drinking rules, and yet another relapse?
She'd gotten her hopes up in the past and watched as I
backed over them on the way down the driveway to the liquor
store.

To describe her as cautiously optimistic when I was in
early sobriety would be an exaggeration. Sheri was just
cautious, and she was curious as to which kind of asshole she
was married to: a drunk one or a sober one.

Her well-placed and necessary caution made her seem
cold and distant to me in many ways. While I appreciated the
support she offered, I was greedy for more. I wanted Sheri to

trade in her caution for enthusiasm. I wanted her to tell me how proud she was and fawn all over me like her liquor-conquering hero. I wanted her to trade her cat-covered flannel pajamas for one of the silk nighties I'd bought her at Victoria's Secret on several overly optimistic trips to the mall over the years. I wanted her to drop her guard and celebrate our new life.

What I didn't understand was that dropping her guard was the worst thing she could do—for her sake and for mine.

The defense mechanisms the loved ones of alcoholics learn to put in place during active alcoholism serve an important purpose. Sheri was adept at reading my moods and intoxication levels and adjusting her communication appropriately. She was a master at maneuvering our kids into activities that kept them clear of me when I was drinking heavily. She knew when to walk away because staying in the same room with me was a recipe for disaster (she didn't always leave when she should have, but at least she knew the difference).

And when I was trying to get sober, Sheri kept all her protections in place. She had no other rational choice. My sobriety was anything but a sure thing, and Sheri was experienced enough to know it. Had she dropped her defenses, forgotten resentments, blindly trusted again and fallen eagerly back in love with me, she would have been setting herself up for a level of pain and disappointment the human brain is not equipped to handle.

Her caution and distance were good for me, too. There's nothing easy about sobriety. I had tried for 10 years to continue my life without a beer in my hand, but without making significant changes. Those attempts at sobriety had failed precisely because of the lack of effort and life-changing

commitment I was willing to put into the endeavor. This time
was different. I was changing everything, and it was as hard as
hell. If my relationship had magically gotten better while
everything else was getting harder, I might have reduced the
intensity of my offensive against the disease. Had Sheri
dropped her defense, success might have seemed too easy. I
needed her to be my supportive but angry ice queen.

The pace of recovery for the loved ones of alcoholics is
necessarily slower than the pace of recovery of us alcoholics.
It just has to be that way. As a drinker trying to break an
addiction, we have to go full speed ahead and throw all of our
energy into the process of sobriety. All the steps in section
two of this book need to become the highest priorities in the
alcoholic's life. That's how the process of quitting drinking
works.

And as important as it is for us alcoholics to have our foot
mashed on the accelerator, it is equally important for our
loved ones to proceed with caution. These two different
paces of recovery are completely logical. But, logical or not,
the resulting misalignment of enthusiasm and trust is yet
another huge challenge for the relationship to navigate.

When I was as excited about my sobriety as Sheri was
unsure of it, connecting as humans, let alone as lovers, was
difficult to say the least. When our attitudes and emotions
were most out of sync, those were the times when I
questioned if my alcoholism was truly to blame for our
troubles. Maybe it wasn't the booze, I would occasionally
think. Maybe she's just a bitch.

Is it any wonder why recovering an alcoholic marriage is
so hard? There we were, lost and afraid, completely unsure
of how to get our marriage back on track, just a sober asshole
and his ice queen bitch.

Blame the Disease

I've heard all the arguments for and against the disease designation for alcoholism, and addiction in general. I'm a believer that because of the chronic nature of alcoholism, and because of the change in brain function that results from excessive drinking, addiction is a neurological disease. Just like cancer, heart disease and type-two diabetes, alcoholism can result from a commitment to bad lifestyle choices and just like those chronic killers, it can be sent into remission with treatment.

I believe alcoholism is a disease. I don't care if you believe it or not. The disease designation is, ultimately, not important. What is important, like make-or-break-your-recovery-and-your-marriage important, is that you blame alcoholism for the destruction it has caused in your life.

Toward the end of my first year of sobriety, I noticed some changes. My anxiety was all but gone and my depression was lessening. I felt little or no need to be in charge and to take control of situations, and I was far less arrogant than I had been as a drinker. I listened as much, or even more than I talked. My stress about the little things was evaporating, and my temper was far less volatile.

Besides providing me with an opportunity to brag about my sober awesomeness, this list of changes makes a critical point. Alcohol was responsible for my anxiety, depression, need for control, arrogance, obnoxiousness, stress and temper. It had to be. When I stopped drinking and stayed sober long enough for my outputs to adjust to my inputs, those maladies all eased.

These changes in my behavior, and the time I took to analyze them, are the single greatest reason I'm able to blame my alcoholic destruction on my alcoholic diagnosis. Sober, I'm not the person who said vile things to my wife. I'm not the person who argued because I was angry without even understanding why. That wasn't me. It was the alcohol. It was the disease.

As I've said consistently, I had to take responsibility for the consequences of my alcoholic behavior. The disease is not an excuse for legal issues, financial collapse, injury, or death caused by an alcoholic. It's not an excuse, but the disease is an explanation that frees the drinker of excessive shame.

Learning that I'm not a diabolical deviant was a huge relief. And it was a relief to Sheri, too.

Just like the loved one of an alcoholic has to recover at a slower pace than the drinker, Sheri was slower to come around to the concept of blaming the disease. That's okay. I don't fault her apprehension. My early sobriety was such a selfish time for me that it was hard for her to determine if I was, or was not, still an asshole. It took well over a year for Sheri to see the changes in me, and for her to adopt the concept of blaming the disease instead of me.

Ultimately, it was just as important a distinction for her recovery as it was for mine. Sheri's reactions to my drinking often turned nasty and volatile. She wasn't proud of her own behavior, either. She felt shame from her reactions and shame for her reluctance to trust that my sobriety would stick this time. When she struggled to trust me, when we had not yet addressed the resentments, when she could barely stand to be in the same room with me, she hated herself for those feelings in the face of all the progress I was making, Had she not been able, eventually, to blame all of it on the disease of alcoholism, her shame would have been paralyzing, and it would have blocked the recovery of our marriage.

We were together for a reason. Under all the pain and years of suffering, there was love. At least, there once had been. The idea that two terrible people married each other to make their united lives miserable just didn't make sense. And it doesn't make sense in your relationship, either. The chances are you're not a terrible person. I'd put down a wager that your life partner isn't the scourge of the earth, either. After living through the turmoil we've survived, I'm confident that the alcohol warped you and your relationship just like it did mine. You and the person you love are not bad people, you just had a very bad thing happen to you. Carrying that shame around will never help. Let it go. Blame the disease and give your relationship a chance.

Timing is important here. Just because I now acknowledge how selfish I was in my first year of recovery doesn't mean I would do it differently if offered a chance to do it all over again. There was a huge hump of neurological dependence to overcome, and selfishness was working to my advantage. With the support of the ice queen, this selfish asshole found permanent sobriety. It worked. I'm blessed and thankful, and I wouldn't change a thing because I know of no other way to get it done.

After that, once I started feeling better, once the anxiety and depression diminished, then it was time for Sheri to start her recovery. In the remaining chapters, I'll describe the painful process we used to recover our marriage. Resentments, helping our kids recover, trust, love, intimacy, patience and professional help; we'll discuss it all. Each step in the process was critically important. There's absolutely no

way our marriage would have survived without carefully
working through it all.

But starting the process had to wait until the necessary
selfishness was over. There is so much to learn, and so many
revelations to experience before the work of marriage
recovery will make any sense.

Make no mistake, the timing is important, but eventually
it was definitely Sheri's turn to prioritize recovery over me. If
we had ignored it, the pain would not have gone away (we
tried that and it didn't work). Just because she went second
does not mean she could have not gone at all. Our marriage
would not have survived.

Sobriety doesn't fix anything, but it is a necessary
prerequisite to a healthy marriage. Love and alcoholism can't
coexist. A sober asshole and an ice queen bitch might be able
to cohabitate, but if you want real and sustained love, you're
going to have to focus on recovery.

chapter 14 | healing the wounds

Alcoholism is a progressive disease in every imaginable way. Once we drink enough that alcohol consumption is affecting the release of our pleasure neurotransmitters, the damage is done, and the hold alcohol has on our lives can only increase. There is no return to moderation, no undoing the impact through drinking less. It is kind of like a bad sunburn. If you are already lobster-red and blistered, SPF 100 lotion is not going to fix your ailment. It's just too late.

The same is true for the damage done in an alcoholic relationship. Once the drinking has a serious impact on the feelings, emotions, communication and trust between two people, limiting booze intake is not a solution. In fact, trying to control our drinking again feels, to the people who love us, a lot like slathering SPF 100 lotion on their blistered sunburn and sending them back out into an exposed, blazing, bikini-clad afternoon.

Resentment

Resentments build on each other. Apologies from an active alcoholic are meaningless, because by continuing to drink, we guarantee that the indiscretion will be repeated. At some point in the relationship, over the objections and denials of the drinker, the spouse connects the dots in indelible ink.

The moodiness, anger, depression, anxiety, meanness, gaslighting, insults, irresponsibility and irrationality are assigned by the loved one of the drinker to either one of two sources. Either the alcohol is to blame, or the drinker is an inherently bad person. Once this connection is made, the apologies are wasted breath. Bad people don't repent. They continue to do bad things. And alcohol isn't going to suddenly do a 180 and start improving the drinker's behavior. "Sorry," becomes meaningless because there is just too much history to be ignored. The behavior pattern becomes clear. The only question is what to do about it.

I'm a believer that there are few, if any, inherently bad people in the world. If you found sufficient positive attributes in a person that it allowed you to fall in love and marry him, there probably isn't a dark sludge sloshing around in the pit of his soul. It's probably the alcohol. The problem is, even once you've determined that alcohol is to blame, the solution to the situation is far more complex than logic would suggest. As we've already discovered, sobriety doesn't fix anything. It is a necessary prerequisite, but sobriety only prevents the building of additional alcoholic resentment. It does nothing about the huge wall of resentment, usually constructed over years and decades of heavy drinking, that is left behind when alcohol leaves the relationship.

About a year into my sobriety, I was feeling quite better. Much of my alcohol-induced depression was finally subsiding as my neural functions returned to near-normal and my anxiety was all but gone. Cravings for alcohol were becoming less severe and less frequent, and much of the shame associated with my drinking and my sobriety was becoming less intense. Personally, my sobriety was having tangible benefits for the first time since my teenage years.

My relationship, however, was another story entirely. The communication between my wife and I was clearly stunted and full of apprehension, there were huge holes in the trust between us and intimacy was a ravaged mess. As I was feeling better, more confident and convinced that my work in sobriety was transforming me, my marriage seemed to be crumbling right before my eyes.

I was ready to leave the past behind us, but my wife just couldn't let it go. At first, I thought this was a character flaw: a personal defect unique to my life partner, her twice-divorced mother and twice-divorced sister. Discontent and a relentless death grip on the past seemed a family trait that was now plaguing my marriage. What I didn't understand at the time was that Sheri's inability to move effortlessly past alcoholic resentments, now that I was sober, had nothing to do with genetics or family history. It was normal. She was behaving like any other human who experiences the trauma of verbal and emotional abuse at the hands of someone she loved.

Sheri wasn't holding onto the past. She wanted desperately to move forward, but the past was holding onto her.

We started spending time each week discussing the pain and resentment that clung to Sheri from the most traumatic of my drunken episodes. We didn't gloss over the specifics talking in generalities and punctuating the conversation with an apology. We talked about the details. We got painfully accurate. In many cases, my memory was foggy at best, because I was in a blackout when my most egregious behavior or vile name calling and viscous lashing out took place.

Much of the detail was new to me. It was impossibly hard to hear. It was like listening to the despicable behavior of someone else, someone unrecognizable and barely human— and then realizing that monster was me.

At first, I didn't understand why we were doing it. Why did we need to go into the excruciating details of the past? Was Sheri getting some joy from hurting me? Was this all about retribution and revenge?

Eventually, I began to absorb what was happening and started to feel the purpose for dredging up the most painful history. Part of moving past the resentment was me apologizing for the specifics of the pain my alcoholism caused. It was not enough to issue a blanket, "sorry." I needed to hear the details and feel and express remorse.

But even more than that, I needed to experience and acknowledge the pain. After years of being told she was wrong, she was crazy, she was stupid and she was to blame, Sheri needed me to confirm her belief that my alcohol-induced ridiculousness was the source of all our misery. My apology was important, but not as important as my awareness of the truth.

As I sat on our front porch, hour after hour, week after week, reliving the horror of my alcoholic past, something started to change between us. As I listened, something new happened. Sure I was sorry, but I had long been sorry. I started to feel deep empathy for the terror of Sheri's life in an alcoholic marriage, our alcoholic marriage that had been tormented by my alcoholism. Her experiences became our shared experiences, and I started to truly understand her pain. Sorry was nice, but it wasn't enough. Understanding and compassion was much deeper and required re-exposing the wounds before they could begin to heal.

I learned a lot through the process of addressing all of Sheri's alcoholic resentments. Above all, I learned that her experiences needed to become our experiences, before working together, healing together and growing together made any sense. Dealing with the past, doing the work and getting dirty with details didn't solve all our marital problems, but it was progress. For the first time in a couple of decades, we were moving together in the right direction.

Impact on our Kids

I was always cautiously optimistic that Sheri and I had worked together effectively to keep most of the trauma of my addiction from affecting our four kids. For the most part, we had. But I underestimated the impact my drinking had on our children in two ways.

First, there had been incidents where Sheri and I had failed to protect our children from the insanity of alcoholism. As part of our resentment processing, Sheri and I identified five specific instances where we had argued loudly and openly, and the kids were undeniably involved. I recognized this pain I had inflicted and was ready to roll up my sleeves and do whatever it would take to fix it.

But an understanding of the rest of the impact of my drinking on our kids was far more elusive to me. Kids are incredibly intuitive, and they are watching and listening even when we are sure they are ignoring us. Even when they dismiss our advice and think they are smarter than us, our words and actions can't help but rub off on them. So, when I thought I was hiding in the basement, drinking and sulking alone, they were all vividly aware of what was going on. I thought they were immersed in their own little lives, but they were also intentionally avoiding me because they knew what it meant when I started making frequent trips to the refrigerator. They might not have been privy to the details, but they could sense the darkness. My children—all children— are far more in tune with, and impacted by, their surroundings than we adults usually realize.

So, much like my wife and I spent countless hours processing her alcoholic resentments, we also spent hours with our kids discussing my disease. First, we went through the details of the five incidents Sheri and I identified. We explained what happened from our perspective, and I apologized most sincerely. Then, we asked them to share their feelings about both my drinking and my sobriety.

The ensuing emotion was raw and abundant. There was anger, fear, confusion and sadness expressed. I watched in stunned silence as our second oldest child held our oldest while she sobbed and shouted at me. We welcomed them to speak freely and assured them that tears were therapeutic. I made no excuses. We made no attempt to rewrite their history and bend their truth. They told us how they felt and shared their pain. Sheri and I absorbed as much of it as we could, and we validated their experiences.

I told them how sorry I was. We explained that from that day forward, nothing was off limits. There would be no more shame or hiding or secrets, and we wanted to know how they were feeling as our family's recovery from alcoholism progressed. We have since shared with our kids all the details about brain chemistry, bibliotherapy, nutrition, patience, emotions and resentment. My kids understand alcoholism better than most adults. They know their parents made mistakes, and they feel our compassion for their pain and confusion. Most of all, they know how much Sheri and I love them.

Our kids are our responsibility. The influence of our behavior is every bit as important as our unconditional love for our children. We decide, by our actions, what kind of adult humans we want to grow and nurture in our little family factories. In sobriety, in recovery, our kids know we will always do everything we can to protect them. We have a unique trust that grows from the survival of addiction.

Trust

Without trust, there is no love in a marriage. Trust is as fundamental as oxygen. There are ways in which the trust between Sheri and me is unshakable, even in the face of active alcoholism. We both love our kids completely. They were always safe, and we always provided for their needs. I never left them waiting on a soccer field, or after band practice, while I sat on a bar stool and neglected my family. As is the case with many high-functioning alcoholics, part of the trust between my wife and I remained intact. Our trust in each other that we would never intentionally or knowingly allow our kids to meet with any harm was one such example of unwavering trust.

We have also always trusted each other to be financially responsible, hardworking, ethical and faithful. Neither financial collapse, nor infidelity, were part of our alcoholic marriage. It is hard to imagine, really, how someone who can lie to everyone around him, including himself, would never dream of cheating or running up our credit cards. Did I spend money we couldn't afford on alcohol? Absolutely, but I always found a different corner to cut to make up the difference. Did I feel unfulfilled in my relationship with my wife? Absolutely, but I never cheated. I never even thought about it, really.

So, there were really important facets of trust that remained strong between us even as our marriage was burning down around us. The trust that we clung to might have been what held us together as the rest of our relationship crumbled, and Sheri lost trust in me in so many other areas.

While she always trusted me to never intentionally harm the kids, she knew that I occasionally drove when I should not have. Sometimes, our kids were in the car when I should not have been behind the wheel. Sheri trusted my intent, but she lost trust in my judgment completely. It is impossible to successfully co-parent with someone when you don't trust his decision-making. Intent is never enough.

If I promised to keep my drinking in check at an event we were attending, Sheri had no faith in my ability to do so. If I told her about the new boundaries I had established to control my drinking, she knew all my rules were destined for violation. On the many occasions when I promised her that I was done drinking for good, she knew that was a promise I was incapable of keeping.

When I raised my voice and called my beloved wife the most vile and vicious of names, she knew it was a mistake to have trusted me with her heart.

Sobriety is the necessary first step. It doesn't fix anything, but an alcoholic marriage can never heal without it. Next comes the need to work through the alcohol-induced resentments. The process is as painful as it is required. There are no shortcuts. The past cannot be left in the past. It must be dragged back into the light of day where all the suffering and harm can be both acknowledged and repented. If the married couple has been blessed with children, their pain and misguidance, both overt and intuitive, must be addressed. Our kids have to know that we love them, and we are committed to never repeating our sins of the past.

Those steps require a lot of humility. After years or decades of denying the severity of the impact alcohol is having on your life, you have to reverse your own opinion and recognize the depth and breadth of the alcoholic destruction. In my case, I went from an arrogant know-it-all, proud to be a successful husband, father and contributing member of society who quite enjoyed drinking adult beverages, to a hopeless alcoholic who was holding onto everything that mattered by my fingernails. I'm not describing a transformation that took place over years as my alcoholism slowly progressed. I'm describing a mental and emotional transformation that took place overnight, as I gave up for the last time and admitted I could endure the pain no longer.

That change, that awareness that my entire life was just one big lie, that sudden realization is what made possible the humility required to move through the process of saving my marriage. But even then, as I owned the behaviors that caused such resentment, and I told my kids the degree to which I had let them down, I still had to face the fact that my wife didn't trust me in so many vitally important ways.

Humility wasn't enough. Apologies, and even forgiveness, were not enough. Honesty, introspection, awakening, realization, understanding, empathy and compassion—all of it combined was not enough to rebuild the trust annihilated by our alcoholic marriage. For the trust to begin to grow, something else was needed.

Patience

When I first started to understand that healing my hijacked, alcoholic brain would take a year or more, I was astonished by the significance of that amount of time. Then, when I was well into my second year of recovery, and my marriage wasn't getting any better, I was angry and confused. But when I put it all in perspective and compared the time I had spent in recovery to the two-and-a-half decades that I drank with reckless abandon, the time required to heal my badly scarred marriage simply made more sense.

You can't wind it up, day after day, beer after beer, for a quarter of a century, and expect to unwind it in a long weekend of heartfelt conversation. It doesn't work like that. Nothing worthwhile recovers from a battering like the abuse a marriage takes from alcoholism and bounces back unscathed.

So, we had something else to add to the relationship recovery list, and this was something my newly learned humility did not equip me to handle. I was getting pretty good at reliving the past and validating my wife's pain. I was actually enjoying developing a new connection with my kids, devoid of deceit and centered on freedom from my oppressive disease. But I had no experience that would prepare me for sitting and waiting for the trust to rebuild.

At the top of the list of things about which my wife did not—could not—trust me, was my commitment to never drink again. She had been disappointed so many times before. Both times I made it to six months of sobriety, I eventually changed my mind and drank. On the occasion that I made it to nine months without alcohol, I violated her faith in me and brought alcohol back into our lives. Believing that this time would be any different was not just beyond the scope of her rational and intelligent mind, it would have been naive and foolish. Just as history had destroyed her love for me, history made trust illogical.

If I said to my wife, "Hey Sheri, I need to talk to you about something," or, "I have something important to tell you," she would lurch into a state of immobilizing panic. Those are the words I used to initiate a conversation about the new drinking rules I had concocted each time I started drinking again. Those words brought back a flood of pain and terror even before she heard the details of what I had to say.

So, deep into our recovery, if I wanted to discuss buying mulch for the front yard or going on a family hike the next weekend, if I used those phrases (or anything similar) to introduce the topic, I sent my wife into a state of shock. No amount of talking or apologizing or understanding could make that terror go away. Sheri just had to endure me starting innocent, non-alcoholic sentences that way, sentences about mulch and hiking and have the conversations not end in life-crushing disappointment. And she had to have that same non-threatening experience over and over for months and years, before her gut reaction to my requests for her attention stopped causing paralysis.

It is not unlike the retraining of the subconscious mind of an alcoholic. After years of drinking alcohol in the evenings, I had to have night after night after night alcohol-free before my brain learned the new plan. Explaining the plan was useless. My subconscious would only be convinced through repetition. Likewise, my wife needed many new, pleasurable experiences to replace the alcoholic horror of the past before she stopped anticipating that horror.

This is really important, and it trips up so many relationships in recovery. They do the hard, proactive work of dealing with resentments. They address the pain inflicted on their kids. All this tireless work is hands-on and moves at whatever pace the couple's tolerance for endured pain will allow. But then, when it is time to wait for the wounds to heal, and to replace bad alcoholic memories with every day, normal, healthy memories of a functional relationship, they give up. What more do you want from me? I've apologized for everything. I've got nothing left to give. The thoughts and words go something like that. All that's left to do is be patient, and sometimes, patience is simply too much to ask.

It's like preparing the soil, planting the seeds, fertilizing and watering a potentially lush garden, then refusing to wait for it to grow. This is trust we're talking about. I had it. I lost it. I was willing to do anything to get it back. Almost anything, it turned out. Waiting was the one thing I wasn't prepared to do. Waiting seemed unacceptably grueling and passive. Waiting for the wounds to heal was as arduous as it was necessary. For me, for many of us in this situation, waiting was the hardest part.

Trust is stubborn and hard-earned. Eventually, I learned patience out of necessity. I became resigned to the fact that there simply wasn't any other way. Trust is special, after all. If it was easy, everyone would do it.

Waiting surely wasn't easy but regaining the trust of my wife was worth the wait.

chapter 15 | drowning intimacy

Sex and intimacy are important in a healthy, thriving marriage. Any survey on relationship struggles will always have "problems in bed" and "infidelity" in the Top 10 list, along with a spouse's refusal to love IndyCars (will this guy ever stop making auto racing references?). We're going to talk about sex now, so I thought maybe a joke would lighten the tension and discomfort. Seriously, stop thinking about race cars and focus. Cheating, and/or forms of sexual dysfunction plague a huge percentage of struggling marriages (I'd give you a statistic, but it turns out, people lie about sex problems, so it would be a wild guess).

Also, consistently in the top 10 reasons marriages fail or struggle is alcohol abuse. Whoa, we've got a double or triple whammy here. Throw in kids and some financial struggles, and it is a wonder how anyone stays married, ever.

Alcoholism and Intimacy Cannot Coexist

I am not familiar with a single example where heavy drinking and thriving intimacy have both survived in a marriage. I believe it to be a definitive statement to say alcoholism and intimacy cannot coexist. They just can't. If you are in an alcoholic marriage, either as the drinker or the loved one, and intimacy has been destroyed by the disease, you are not to blame. Drowning intimacy is a thing, and it has happened millions (maybe billions) of times over the centuries. You might be special in many ways, but your intimacy failure in your alcoholic marriage isn't one of them.

I have good news. My wife and I are living proof that this condition can be reversed and thriving intimacy can be restored. But it takes an enormous amount of work, and even more patience. Before you can fix it, you have to understand what happened in the first place.

We believe there are two directions a couple can take toward their alcoholic intimacy dysfunction. Both are very common, and the process of restoring intimacy is similar regardless of which of these two dark paths your sex life has drifted down.

In many alcoholic marriages, sex just stops. Often the drinker is frustrated, the loved one is emotionally unfulfilled, and physical contact becomes repulsive for one or both people in the relationship. The decision to stop having sex can be a mutually agreed upon conclusion, it can be a one-way demand (sometimes associated with an ultimatum), or it can be an unspoken condition that just sort of becomes the norm and is ignored with the efficiency only participants in an alcoholic marriage have mastered.

How sex comes to an end is really rather unimportant. Since alcoholic marriages are bastions of lies and deceit anyway, it is rather unlikely that an honest evaluation of the sexual dysfunction is possible while the drinker is drinking. That a drinker would choose alcohol over sex is not at all surprising for anyone familiar with the disease of addiction. That the drinker would openly admit a preference to booze over his wife is, however, highly unlikely. And if he did, well, that would be a horrible thing to say. So, talking about the whole mess during active alcoholism is likely to be more heartbreaking than helpful.

If this is your situation, there is a silver lining to the cloud of crusty touchless-ness. By eliminating intimacy and sex from your relationship, you have stopped doing damage in at least this one specific aspect of your dysfunctional alcoholic marriage. Healing from nothing is a bit easier and less time consuming that healing from something bad. You don't have a deep hole to climb out of just to get to nothing, you are already there. If you want a new car, it is better to trade in an old, unused one than to try to trade one you've wrecked into a bridge embankment over and over again. Unfortunately, a sexless marriage devoid of intimacy was not our problem.

Sheri and I smashed that old jalopy into so many immovable objects, that repairing our love and romance seemed impossible. We had "the other" intimacy problem. We continued to have loveless sex with despicable regularity even after intimacy was a distant memory.

Sex, Booze and a Very Rocky Road

Sex has always been a featured component of our relationship right from the start. When we met in college, we were both big drinkers. As is typical of relationships that start out floating along on a river of booze, we didn't wait long to start exploring each other's bodies on a regular basis. There was certainly passion in the beginning felt by both of us. We were falling in love, and our bodies seemed to fit together as though we were made for each other.

Looking back, the hottest time between us physically was nothing less than the unknown beginning of our own intimate undoing. Alcohol lubricated all the emotional discomfort that comes with getting to know someone and deciding if it is a good fit. Long walks in the park, afternoons spent holding hands, and talking about the future, sharing hopes, dreams, fears and insecurities...yeah, we didn't do any of that. We drank booze at parties, went home together and had sex. It was wonderful, but we had no idea the steps we were skipping and the damage our routine would cause for us down the road.

Marriage began to seem inevitable. We thought we had it all: we laughed, we drank, we were both hard workers and the sex was full of passion and mutual pleasure. That was love, right? If there was more to growing up and settling down, we didn't know it. I was offered a job right out of college that provided us security and allowed Sheri to continue exploring her culinary passion, both educationally and with lots of employment opportunities.

We fought too much and we both drank a lot, but in our early 20s, we were unable to draw the correlation. Our relationship was never perfect, and we had more than a few nights that left us both deeply troubled in the morning. Still, it is impossible to fix what we didn't understand. We did love each other. Deeply. We were making our young relationship work, though doing so was harder than either of us expected. We kept drinking. We kept having sex. I never doubted that it would all work out.

And there was romance. I proposed on a snow drift overlooking Lake Superior, on a cliff above Duluth, Minnesota. We had the finest hotel suite in town that night, and we drank champagne and made love until we could physically take no more of either. There was no hesitation when Sheri accepted my proposal. We both knew we had problems, but we had not yet made the connection between our disagreements and alcohol. We were flawed, but perfection was never the goal.

We were married in the summer of 1997. The night before our wedding was one of the worst of our lives. This is a story so shameful; it has never been told before. I started the evening at the bars with my groomsmen. Sheri was with her bridesmaids out on the town as well. We met up, and the bridal party drank together without a care in the world. What had all the potential to be an epic night of celebration, Sheri and I surrounded by our best friends, began to unravel over some dispute so trivial I can't possibly recall what it was.

We started arguing. We separated from the party to continue our drunken fight. Sheri was supposed to drive the 20 minutes to her mother's house that night. I was supposed to join the groomsmen back at the hotel. Instead, we fought and drank until we were kicked out of the bar after 3 a.m. But that wasn't the end of it. We both had more illogical hate to spew. We checked into a hotel together so we could fight until dawn.

Nothing ever got resolved that night. No one won. No one apologized. We simply ran out of time. On the morning of what was supposed to be the best day of our lives, we both retreated to our separate corners, and carried on with the planned festivities. We were married that afternoon, both full of doubt from the night before. Sometimes, God or the universe is screaming at you, and you are too stubborn or proud to listen to the message. This was one of those times. The only thing that allowed the ceremony to take place that painful and warped afternoon is that we'd both grown accustomed to the insanity. The way we treated each other should have been a deal breaker. Because of its familiarity, we carried on.

I'm not saying that our marriage was a mistake. I could not possibly be happier or more in love with my wife. I'm saying I made two-and-a-half decades of our life together far harder than it had to be. I think the message that we missed was not one of incompatibility. It was a flashing red light about the disaster drinking was for our relationship.

The first inkling that my drinking was a problem occurred to Sheri as I came home from work every evening, night after night and poured a drink. It seemed abnormal to her to drink every night. Drinking was for weekend partying. Weeknight drinking was gluttonous and unnecessary. It is a stretch to say that she understood the connection between my drinking and our arguments, but she was growing increasingly aware that something was wrong.

The more I drank, the less interest Sheri had in alcohol. Two things were happening: Sheri was maturing, thinking about children and her career, and finding it harder to fit alcohol into her adult lifestyle. Also, my consistent and excessive drinking was beginning to repulse my bride. I always smelled like beer or whiskey, I was barely coherent at the end of most nights, and Sheri's place in the pecking order behind alcohol was becoming increasingly apparent. I just wasn't attractive, and Sheri began to question her decision to dedicate her life to me.

But one thing did not change even as I became less and less attractive to my wife: consistent sex. We still had sex quite regularly, although it began to be totally one-sided. It's not that I was no longer willing to help Sheri find pleasure in sex. Her feelings of disgust for me turned a physical act of love into an obligation. Sheri felt a duty to perform in the way she always had, but finding joy in the act just became a mysterious impossibility. She did it. She didn't get anything out of it, but she didn't refuse, either.

I could tell it wasn't the same. I could tell something was wrong. But to be quite blunt, I was getting what I needed and my constant alcohol consumption left me mentally incapable of digging any deeper. Yes, I wanted my wife to desire me, but that longing slowly faded away, and figuring that out, while still important to me, was third on my list behind my drinking and my sexual satisfaction. It's like when someone regularly has chest pain but ignores it and hopes it goes away. I could see I was doing damage to my marriage, but I was too ignorant and naive to do anything about it.

The Agreement

As the years went by, my drinking continued and Sheri's disgust for me physically grew. Rather than take a step back and try to evaluate our failing intimate relationship, I did what all good alcoholics do. I ignored the problem and pressed harder to get exactly what I wanted. I convinced Sheri that inconsistency was a liability. I told her that not knowing if I was or was not getting some when I went to bed filled me with anxiety. We were experiencing a great deal of stress in the business that we ran together, and Sheri genuinely wanted to help me relax and feel optimistic about our future. So she agreed to my request to perform some kind of sexual act every night. "The Agreement," as we often referred to it, seemed brilliant and totally consoling to me at the time. What I didn't realize was that over the years it was in effect, it would do more damage to our intimate relationship than anything else imaginable.

I thought my needs were being met. I was far too deeply in love with alcohol to understand how important Sheri's sexual satisfaction actually was to me. I thought that as long as I got mine, I had created a perfect situation. Meanwhile, Sheri grew to completely loath any and all physical contact with me. Not only was orgasm wildly out of the question for her, but even my fingers touching her skin made her recoil and seethe with anger and frustration.

Let me be clear that I never, ever wanted to hurt my wife. While she was falling out of love with me, I continued to love her deeply. The Agreement was the concoction of a warped, alcoholic mind. It seemed to solve a problem of uncertainty that my booze-soaked brain was incapable of managing. I was simply not in a position to understand the damage I was doing. It was not intentional. The Agreement is one of my most significant life regrets (and I have a lot of them).

While I don't expect anyone to feel sorry for me for my ignorance, I do think this is a critically important component of our story, for people in similar situations, to understand. The alcoholic brain is selfish, both when intoxicated and when sober. It comes down to a simple balancing of pros versus cons. I knew The Agreement was hurting my wife and weakening our bond, but my sexual satisfaction seemed pivotal to my ability to sleep and do the exhausting work I needed to do in our business. Was it selfish? Absolutely. Did it feel that way at the time? Only partially, because I truly believed the work I was doing was for the good of the family. And I didn't think I could do that work without getting my needs met at almost any cost.

I was wrong in so many ways. I am not making any excuses, but the explanation might help you navigate your relationship. Looking back through the lens of long-term sobriety, I feel like I was a sexual predator. At the time, I felt justified and loving. I always offered to return the favor sexually, and I wasn't intuitive enough to understand the devastating message her constant refusals were delivering. There is one more despicable thing. The Agreement didn't end with my sobriety. I still felt I needed the release, and was justified in expecting it, well over a year into my recovery. For much of that time, I understood the degree to which a couple decades of bad alcoholic sex had destroyed intimacy in my marriage. What I couldn't understand was the key to moving forward.

In the ultimate display of selfishness, I didn't want to dissolve The Agreement because I felt I had already given up so much. I had stopped drinking. I was making such a profound sacrifice, that I didn't think it was fair for me to give up my nightly satisfaction as well. I wouldn't say I felt like Sheri owed the constant sex to me, but I did feel justified in accepting her willingness to hold up her end of the bargain. Even over a year into my recovery, there was still so much I didn't understand.

As for Sheri's perspective on our sexual situation, she was repulsed by everything almost to a point of numbness. Her perspective on right or wrong had been so badly twisted and mangled, and she had ignored her intuition for so long, that she was unable to pull us back from the edge of destruction. She knew it was warped, but she couldn't dissect the deviant from the natural. Sex in any and all forms, with any degree of frequency, had become disgusting. She felt tremendous guilt for not standing up to me and making demands. A huge part of the problem was that she didn't know what to demand. Normal or natural was beyond her grasp, too.

The Feeling is Mutual

So well into recovery from my alcoholism, as we were trying desperately to breathe life back into our marriage, I was still, through The Agreement, suffocating our hopes for intimacy. The key to starting the process of reversing the sexual damage done resided in my own healing neurochemistry. As my brain healed, and my dopamine release returned to near normal, Sheri's lack of pleasure in bed started to become a real challenge. It became a real challenge for me.

I was learning to process real human emotions. I was figuring out how to feel good, and trying to avoid feeling bad, without any input from a brain-function hijacking poison. It was like numbness wearing off after leaving the dentist's office. The more I learned to process emotion, the more important it became to me that Sheri feel pleasure from our sex. I began to feel slimy in my predatory skin, and I didn't like that at all.

I was sober. I was putting some serious distance between me and my active addiction. But I was still a monster in one distinct and painful way. That had to stop.

Just as sobriety doesn't fix anything in an alcoholic marriage, ending The Agreement was a necessary prerequisite, but no solution at all. We stopped doing further damage, but there was enough twisted rubble of sexual dysfunction to last a lifetime.

Sheri would have been content to give up on intimacy as permanent collateral damage from my disease. She wasn't particularly interested in fixing the problem. She thought perhaps amputation (figuratively...maybe literally, too) would allow us to best fix the other problems in our marriage as our relationship recovery continued.

My recognition that Sheri's pleasure sexually was required for my sexual satisfaction was a turning point of sorts for both of us. It was the first unselfish intimate expression I'd offered in many, many years. Sheri didn't so much appreciate it at first. She saw it as yet another sexual requirement placed firmly on her shoulders. "Now I have to not only do it, but also find a way to enjoy it?" she asked in frustration. But she did recognize it as different and saw that it was a desire from me to be generous. That meant a lot. It didn't make navigating our way back to intimacy easy, but it was an indication that we were finally going in the right direction.

This change in my mental approach to our mutual sexual pleasure also meant our frequency of performance was dramatically reduced. It made me feel like a vulture to have sex when Sheri wasn't into it. This is exactly how a horny spouse is supposed to feel. If it wasn't good for both of us, it just wasn't going to happen. As my brain healed, I gradually began to prefer no sex to bad sex at the considerable relief to us both. That is not to say that Sheri never offered to be generous when she wasn't feeling frisky herself. That generosity was in and of itself an act of intimate love. When I could feel that from her, I was grateful and satisfied. That is a very different feeling from one of obligation.

I wasn't the only one changing as we tried to pull our intimate relationship out of the ditch. Sheri recognized that if it was going to happen for us, she was going to have to make a considerable amount of effort. She started looking for ways to relax before bed. We both knew that intimacy was not just all about sex. Intimacy, especially for Sheri, started hours, days and even a week before we pulled back the sheets. How were we communicating with each other? Was there sensual touch that didn't lead to me getting off as we moved through the world together? Did my interactions with our kids warm her heart? Did my mood make her want to spend time alone with me?

Listen, I know that there are women who desire large quantities of sex and find orgasm easy to attain. But I also know my wife is quite representative of most married women with children and other responsibilities. It takes effort to find pleasure from sex. The effort is not a bad thing. This isn't a criticism. Quite to the contrary. The effort makes the sex all the more satisfying and meaningful...for Sheri and for me. Love, satisfaction and meaningfulness—that's where intimacy thrives.

We were making progress through mutual understanding and a common goal. It wasn't about me getting some. It wasn't about Sheri feeling obligated to say yes, or feeling guilty for saying no. It wasn't about my stress relief or Sheri's dutiful instinct. It was about us both working hard to align our souls and our intentions. Do you remember when I explained that when we first met, our bodies just seemed to fit together? It was starting to feel that way again.

It All Comes Down to Patience, Always

As with all aspects of recovery, this is the part that most often trips people up. No one is more into instant gratification than the person who drinks poison to make their discomfort immediately go away. As a result, no one is less equipped to successfully accomplish the hardest part of recovery than a sober alcoholic. Patience is required, and there simply is no shortcut.

Patience is a huge component of beating the cravings to drink in early sobriety. Patience is required to learn to process feelings and ride the unfamiliar wave of emotions. Learning about brain chemistry and regenerating neurotransmitters doesn't happen overnight. Dismantling resentments, building trust and replacing anger and doubt with love and respect all take inordinate amounts of patience.

And once all that is done, after love and trust are restored, you finally have the foundation upon which intimacy and the physical manifestation of love can be built. Not so fast, my eager friends. Even then, intimacy gets to take her own sweet time, too.

Certainly, it is logical that rebuilding intimacy in a sexless marriage is a smoother proposition than first cleaning up the mess made of a relationship where routine sex continued unabated even when love and intimacy were nowhere to be found. Either way, the process cannot be rushed.

While it is our experience that nothing can speed the process along, there are things that can be done to make rebuilding intimacy smoother and even more fun.

Here are some tips to consider once your foundation of love and trust is ready to be elevated to the intimate level:

Romance. If your relationship started like most, alcohol was involved from the beginning. Why not take this sober redo as an opportunity to do things right? Why not make romantic gestures toward each other with no expectation for sex? In our relationship, the gestures don't need to be expensive or elaborately planned. Just something nice, that is not a form of bribery with an expected sexual payout, lights a fire in our relationship that can be turned into a blaze later.

Tender Touch. Again, free from expectation, how about giving each other back rubs? What about a brush of the hand or touch of the cheek as you walk past? Take it from my dreadful experience, grabbing your wife's boobs as you cross a room doesn't count, and can send your intimate growth reeling backwards. But a gentle touch that does not lead to thrusting and humping puts some serious fuel in the intimacy tank.

Buildup. As mentioned earlier in this chapter, intimacy starts long before you enter the bedroom. If you want to have a close, physical relationship, your words matter. Teasing each other has a place, but limit it and make sure it is more than offset by kind remarks and compliments. My wife was not very good at accepting compliments. She had an innate fear that when someone said something nice to her, they must want something. She has worked hard to accept compliments as they are intended, free from attachments. Now, they bring her emotionally closer to me, and make us feel like a team rather than like we are adversaries.

Straight Talk. This tip was the hardest for us to employ in our relationship. An alcoholic marriage has years of baggage from deceit and denials. Honesty was so elusive, that talking openly was at first a challenge sometimes. But the better we got about discussing our honest emotions without regard for the impact our words would have on each other, the better our communication and intimate relationship got. There is more to this one, though. The blunt honesty worked best when it carried into our sexual relationship, too. Sheri was so used to viewing sex as something to hurry up and finish, that she struggled to tell me what felt good, or the things she wanted me to do.

It can be embarrassing to talk about sex, even with our intimate partners. Many of us are only accustomed to talking in vivid detail when we've been drinking. Getting the most out of sober sex required communication, both physical and verbal.

There is no right or wrong way to rebuild intimacy on the foundation of love and trust in a marriage. Go slow and find your way. One thing is for sure, though. Intimacy after alcohol takes time. Be patient, and give your relationship the start it deserved, and maybe never got, when alcohol was center stage. If it was quick and easy, everyone would do it. If it was quick and easy, you wouldn't be reading this book.

Just remember, quick and easy is what got you into this jam in the first place.

chapter 16 | evolve insecurity into instinct

Recovery for an alcoholic seems binary, like a yes or no question. Did I get sober or didn't I? We all know it is much more complicated than that. No one wants to be a "dry drunk" and scuffle through the world angry and feeling deprived. Alcoholism recovery is perplexing, and we've spent the last 60 thousand words explaining that. But for the outsiders looking into our alcoholic relationships, it does seem simple. Is the alcoholic still drinking alcohol or not?

For the loved one of an alcoholic, there is no litmus test of success. From the outside, there is no way to detect a successful recovery versus the continued pain and suffering of being stuck. Likewise, there is no sense of urgency related to the recovery of the loved ones. If the alcoholic doesn't find a solution, he could kill someone or destroy the family. If the loved one doesn't recover, she continues in isolated suffering with what seems like limited collateral damage.

When I was drinking, our lives and our marriage were a mess—full of deceit and lacking trust. When the time came for sobriety, I poured everything I had into my recovery. When our marriage continued to crumble in sobriety, we turned our attention to recovering our marriage, and addressed the resentment, our children, trust, love and intimacy. We slowed the bleeding, but still, something was wrong. We weren't really getting better.

Do you see what was missing? Can you pick out the piece of this complicated puzzle that we inadvertently ignored?

What about Sheri's recovery?

I'm not talking about the work we did to fix our marriage. I'm talking about the work my wife needed to do to fix herself.

Prioritizing the Loved One's Recovery

Alcoholism changes us—all of us, drinkers and second-hand drinkers alike. Some of the effects are permanent. Some of the damage is fixable, but none of it is really reversible. One of the reasons I don't like the term "recovery," is because there is no going back to some place or time in our previous existence. We don't really recover to some state of former selfness. We grow. We evolve. We become enlightened. That is healing and it is full of hope and inspiration, but it is not a return to who we were. Too much has happened. That return is impossible.

The healing, the evolving, the enlightenment—it all takes work. For the loved ones of alcoholics, the idea of working on themselves is amazingly hard to grasp. After years or decades of managing the problems the alcoholism caused, holding the family together, protecting and nurturing the children and suppressing feelings in an attempt to avoid conflict and confrontation, turning the attention inward takes some serious effort and encouragement.

Sheri avoided her recovery for years. It was not a matter of stubbornness or ignorance, at least not eventually. At first, she definitely dealt with anger at the very idea that she had work to do. She wasn't the drunk who had ruined things over and over. It was maddening to think she needed to change or fix anything. But her understanding of the disease of addiction, and the impact my alcoholism had on all of us, brought her around to the realization that we all needed to change in order to find peace and health. Once the anger was gone, it was just a matter of prioritization.

Nothing made Sheri's need to recover more glaringly obvious than our sober ability to still reach the depths of conflicted despair like we did when I was drinking. The simplest disagreement about the most inconsequential of topics sent us reeling. I'm not just talking about the first few months of my sobriety. It was still happening years after I took my last drink.

We had dealt with the resentments. We had rebuilt a lot of trust, and our love was starting to really flourish. We were even making progress on our intimate relationship. But Sheri had not turned her attention on herself. Her reactions, her insecurities and her doubt were draped over our marriage like a cold, wet blanket.

One spring, we were doing yard work together, and I asked Sheri why she was using a compostable paper leaf bag rather than a plastic trash bag. There was no anger in my voice, I wasn't condescending and I made no demands. It was a question. Saving the less accessible paper bags for the fall seemed like a good idea to me, but I wasn't particularly invested in her decision. I was curious, so I asked.

That question led to two miserable weeks for both of us. Just as an alcoholic brain never forgets what to do with alcohol if it is ever reintroduced during relapse, a loved one's brain never forgets how bad it feels to be questioned by the alcoholic. When I was drinking, my questions were loaded with condescension, anger, frustration and disrespect. "Why are you using that bag? What, are you stupid?" That is not what I said, but that is what Sheri heard.

Gaslighting is an unavoidable component of active alcoholism. The only way I could convince Sheri (and myself,

for that matter) that my drinking was normal, was to convince
her that her instincts and feelings were abnormal. No one
wants to make someone they love feel stupid, not even an
active alcoholic. But, when facing my problem and giving up
the alcohol I loved was the only conceivable alternative to
Sheri being wrong, I had to convince her that she was either
ignorant or crazy. I never thought about it like that on a
conscious level. But by denying what she was seeing was in
fact happening, I was sowing the seeds of doubt, and even
hatred.

All the venom lived in Sheri, right below the surface, even
years into my sobriety, waiting to again poison our
relationship upon the asking of even the most innocent of
questions. "Why are you using that bag, Sheri?" was received
as an attack on her intelligence and sanity. Her answer wasn't
an answer at all. It was a counterattack launched on an enemy
who had long since surrendered.

It sounds like I'm trying to blame Sheri here. It sounds
like a jaded alcoholic who can't find the strength to admit his
own destruction. That's not at all what I'm trying to do. This
is another reason why it is so important to recognize
alcoholism as the disease it is, and to blame the disease. Sheri
is the most loving and compassionate person I've ever met.
She is not mean nor evil, and I'm not blaming her for her
response. My alcoholism changed how her brain reacted to
being questioned. She didn't do anything wrong. Just as my
neurotransmitter release changed under heavy alcohol
consumption in my brain's quest for equilibrium, Sheri's
brain adapted to the years of gaslighting. Her brain was
warped by alcohol, too. Instead of processing a question like
a question, she received my inquiry as an act of hostility.
It wasn't her fault, but it was her job to fix the problem.

Sheri has a very natural nurturing instinct. In dealing with my alcoholism, she learned techniques to protect our children and try to save me from myself. Protecting our family was always mama's job, even when I made her work impossible. In both her natural instincts and her learned behavior, the focus of Sheri's attention was always on the people around her; she was caring for our needs and picking up the pieces when I made a mess. At no point in her daily activities did she care for herself. The idea of working on her own mental health was not instinctual. She did not recognize the need because the concept was beyond her outward-facing attention on the people she loves.

This is a nearly universal limitation of the loved ones of alcoholics. They are all great at fixing things, but they are ashamed, angry and unaware of the need to turn their attention on themselves. Prioritizing her recovery was nearly impossible for Sheri. She did not lack the understanding of the importance of active recovery. She lacked the experience and confidence to focus on what she needed.

Insecurities and Instincts

All humans deal with insecurities in various forms. Low self-esteem, lack of confidence, worries about the future, stress, anxiety and the aftermath of trauma...they all come down to a belief that we are not secure in our situations. The way we deal with our insecurities has a huge impact on our successful navigation of our time on this spinning orb.

Drinkers use booze to silence our insecurities. "I have a couple of drinks to relax and unwind." That sounds innocent and normal enough, but relaxing is the relief of anxiety, stress, worry, fear, lack of confidence and the terror of low self-esteem. When we drink to find that relief, what we are really doing is introducing a toxin into our brains to suppress naturally occurring feelings and emotions. There is nothing innocent or natural about stunting our emotional stability and poisoning our coping mechanisms. Drinking isn't managing stress. Alcohol deceives us into believing the insecurities aren't real. When the alcohol leaves our systems, the insecurities are there, more daunting and imposing than ever, and we've done nothing to learn how to tame the beast. So, we drink again. Remember, alcoholism is a progressive disease. Without our human insecurities, there would be no addiction.

The people who love alcoholics have the opposite experience with insecurities and alcohol. And they, too, have naturally occurring human insecurities. Instead of temporarily quieting them, the alcohol they experience second-hand actually makes their insecurities much worse.

In active alcoholism, I doubted Sheri's decision-making, told her that her instincts about my drinking were wrong, and left her bewildered about how she could have so misjudged my character and married me. Her insecurities swelled to an unmanageable size. I took her normal insecurities and made them worse through my defense of my abuse of alcohol. Humans partner up like many members of the animal kingdom. The reasons for finding a partner include procreation, but also comfort and security. By marrying an alcoholic, Sheri chose a partner who would make her feel less secure. I'm not talking about money or physical safety. I'm talking about mental and emotional security.

When it came to feeling safe in her own head, Sheri would have been better off without me.

As a husband who loves my wife very much and views her protection as a big part of my responsibility, that's a tough admission to make. I know I cannot hold myself responsible for another person's happiness—but, that me and my disease are responsible for my wife's gargantuan insecurities is among the greatest regrets of my life (and I've got a lot of regrets). I know what it's like to feel bad, desperately depressed, and bringing that feeling on someone else is no good at all and completely unjustifiable. So you just have a couple of drinks to relax, huh? I wonder if it can ever be as simple as that sounds.

When our insecurities grow out of control, they silence our instincts. I believe people are generally good with loving intentions. I don't believe any of us are born evil. Our instincts are what guide us to make compassionate decisions, with the overall well-being of those in our sphere of influence in mind. When our insecurities grow to levels of hostility, we hurt the ones we love, and disregard the impact on those around us. We react. We can't hear our instincts. We are too scared to listen.

When I was drinking away my insecurities, they came raging back in moments of sober clarity. Much of my arrogant, egotistical actions were born from latent insecurity that I refused to acknowledge and would rather drink away. I never lied on purpose. Never. I never insulted my wife or denied her truth. I couldn't hear the desires of my heart to support and love her. Those desires, those instincts, were constantly drowning in alcohol.

Even more tragically, Sheri's insecurities silenced her instincts. She knew I was drinking too much. She knew that alcohol everyday wasn't healthy and that I was doing damage to our relationship. She knew it, but I put so much doubt in her mind, that she lost confidence in believing her own instincts.

Sheri erected walls and defense mechanisms, and she learned to fire back when questioned. She developed skills in returning venomous insults when she received them from my intoxication. She learned to be angry. She learned to fight back. She learned not to trust me, and she learned that her love for me was misguided. None of that was natural. As her insecurities grew, she learned to ignore her instincts. Almost completely.

Sheri has said repeatedly on our Untoxicated Podcast that she always knew that deep down, I was a good person. She stayed with me because she believed I would find my way home to her. That was her instinct, gasping for air and trying to be heard. We had no idea how to get from where we were to where we are today, but Sheri always believed that if we could figure it out, it would be worth the effort. That's why she had the strength to stay. Her strongest, barely audible instinct told her not to leave me.

Recovery for the loved ones is essentially about a return to a trust in instincts. Sheri had to move past the aggressive and defensive reactions she had learned, and back into a comfort with her own judgment and intentions. She had to learn to accept my questions as they were intended, without malice or passive aggressive intent. She had to learn to trust me.

Just as importantly, she had to learn to trust herself again. Rebuilding self-confidence and quieting the insecurity, that took effort and patience.

Echoes of Recovery

Connection is both absolutely required, and the thing most missing in our society when it comes to the recovery of second-hand drinkers. When you love an alcoholic in recovery, be prepared for frequent questions about how sobriety is going for the drinker. But don't expect anyone to ask you how you are doing, how your recovery from the deadly and chronic disease is coming along. Support for the loved ones is as necessary as it is elusive.

As I wrote about our relationship, and as Sheri and I talked about it on our Untoxicated Podcast, we began to realize how vast the void is in this space. The connection the loved ones desire and require is nonexistent. So many people thank us for telling our story, but those people have no outlet for their own stories.

Many of them do not want a 12-Step program that treats alcoholism as a spiritual deficiency. They don't want to sit across from a therapist and listen to recommendations for handling their spouses. They want connection. They want to be heard. They want a safe place where empathy is genuine, and compassion is given and received generously.

Sheri and I created Echoes of Recovery to fill that void. The loved ones of alcoholics are the focus, and our mission is all about connection. Our participants tell their stories and resonate with the stories of others to great mutual benefit. In this program, we hear the echoes of our similar stories, and we find strength and healing together.

EchoesOfRecovery.com

If you love an alcoholic, sobriety is not enough for either of you. The relationship needs repair for sure, but so do you individually, as well. It is long and hard and tiring and often dreary. Recovering from alcoholism often feels hopeless, and it seems you are taking two steps back for every step you take forward. I hate the rainbows and unicorns in the recovery community, so I won't sugar coat it. Recovery is likely to be the hardest thing you'll ever accomplish.

But if you prioritize your mental health, and you prioritize your relationship, you can make it. You can heal and recover. You can make progress in weakening the power of your insecurities. You can learn to listen to your instincts again. You can find the enlightenment only available to those of us who peer over the cliff of tragedy, and slowly back away from the edge.

You can evolve. Evolve from the misguided belief that alcohol has benefits when used in moderation. Evolve from the shame-filled stigma of both alcoholism and recovery. Evolve, from the person who fell victim to an addictive poison, into the best possible version of yourself. Evolve into the elusive contentment we all deserve.

Sheri and I aren't done evolving. Not by a long shot. But we're going the right direction, finally, after so many years of betrayal and sabotage. It feels good. It is still messy and imperfect, but we are doing it together. We have found something worth holding onto.

That's our story. If it resonates, if you understand our pain and can feel our hope, maybe you can find it, too. We hope you'll join us with your own soberevolution.

| acknowledgments

I feel undying love and gratitude for my writing coach and dear friend, Shari Caudron. Shari taught me so much about digging deep and telling a compelling story. She helped me with structural issues in my writing, but even more than that, she taught me that vulnerability is a unique gift to be treasured and shared. Most of all, Shari was the first person "from the business" to give me confidence that I could write.

I feel such deep affection for and allegiance to my editor, Julie "Jules" Balsiger, who sweated through every detail with me. In addition to editing, Jules is responsible for the layout and cover design work on this book. She is as caring and mission driven as she is talented, and I am very thankful to have Jules in my life.

I am thankful to all my friends at Stone Soup Publishing, and I'm especially grateful for their dedication to changing the way our society views alcohol.

I absolutely love working with The Addiction Nutritionist, Kelly Miller. I thank her for her contribution to my understanding of this disease, her partnership in battling the stigma and her friendship. Please look for my second book, with Kelly as my co-author, from Stone Soup Publishing in 2021.

This is my first of many books. I am blessed to know these loving and inspiring people will stick with me as we crush the stigma associated with alcoholism.

We will continue to lead this soberevolution together.

| about the author

Matt Salis is the executive director of the Denver, Colorado-based nonprofit, Stigma [theStigma.org]. Among the programs run by Stigma are SHOUT Sobriety [SHOUTSobriety.com] for alcoholics in early recovery and Echoes of Recovery [EchoesOfRecovery.com] for the loved ones of alcoholics.

To make a fully tax-deductible donation to Stigma, to be a part of the solution and keep this mission going, please visit theStigma.org/donate.

Matt lives with his four children and his wife, Sheri, who was a vital contributor to every word in this book. Together, they believe recovery from alcoholism is just the first critical step to living an enlightened and faithful life of service.

'Cause that's where the happy is.

Made in the USA
Monee, IL
26 September 2021